# Finding Your Niche:
# 12 Keys to
# Opening God's Doors for
# Your Life

# FINDING YOUR NICHE:
## 12 KEYS TO OPENING GOD'S DOORS FOR YOUR LIFE

Paul L. King, D.Min., Th.D.

WORD & SPIRIT PRESS

Unless otherwise designated, Scripture is taken from the HOLY BIBLE, NEW INTERNATIONAL VERSION. Copyright © 1973, 1978, 1984, International Bible Society. Used by permission of Zondervan Bible Publishers.

Scripture quotations marked as NASB are taken from the New American Standard Bible®, Copyright © 1960, 1962, 1963, 1968, 1971, 1972, 1973, 1975, 1977, 1995 by The Lockman Foundation. Used by permission. (www.Lockman.org)

Scripture quotations marked as KJV are taken from the Holy Bible, King James Version.

Published in Tulsa, Oklahoma, by Word & Spirit Press
WordSP@gmail.com • http://WandSP.com

Book design and composition by Bob Bubnis / Booksetters, Bowling Green, Kentucky

ISBN 10: 0-9785352-8-6 [paperback]
ISBN 13: 978-0-9785352-8-5

♾ The paper used in this publication meets the minimum requirements of the American National Standard for Information Sciences—Permanence of Paper for Printed Library Materials, ANSI Z39.48-1992.

# Contents

Dedicated to
those throughout my life
who helped me to find my niche

# Acknowledgements

I have dedicated this book to the mentors, coaches, and spiritual directors throughout my life who have helped me to find my niche. **Jerry McCauley**, my pastor as a teenager, gave me my first opportunities to preach at the age of 17. Retired evangelist **Roland Gray, Sr.**, now with the Lord, was like a grandfather to me in the ministry. I sat at his feet as a 19 year old (actually on a chair in his study) and drank in of the wisdom of 50 years of ministry. Pastor **Ron MacDonald** took me on as his assistant as a 20 year old and discipled me in many aspects of ministry, patient with my youthful immaturity, and rebuking me when necessary. I called on him for counsel for many years following. Decades later when he was a missionary in South Africa he gave me opportunity to preach in a Zulu church and teach in an African Bible college.

Pastor and missionary **Cal McCarter** has been both a friend and mentor through the years who has also given wise words of encouragement and rebuke. **Rev. Ernie Gruen** mentored me through some tough times in ministry and personal struggle, providing insight and encouragement. Late Oral Roberts University professor **Dr. Charles Farah**, who himself had been discipled by Navigators leader Lorne Sanny, spent two years discipling me weekly, challenging me intellectually and spiritually, and mutually memorizing Bible verses together. The late **Dr. K. Neill Foster**, former publisher of Christian Publications, taught me the ropes of the writing, editing and publishing industry. Pastor friends **Jim Garrett** and **Bill Sullivan** have provided counsel, intellectual stimulation, and spiritual insight through the years. **Dr. Mark Roberts**, friend and colleague, has provided further mentoring insights in writing. Most important of all, my wife Kathy has patiently and lovingly given me much insight and spiritual direction through our 32+ years of marriage and for this book.

# Introduction

*"The thing is to understand myself, to see what God really wants
me to do; . . . to find the idea for which I can live and die."*
—Søren Kierkegaard

*"I have given you the keys to the kingdom of heaven"*
(Matthew 16:19).

I felt like a square peg in a round hole. In the early 1980s I was a northeast-ern suburban intellectual serving as pastor of a rural community church in a tiny Colorado cowboy town. I just did not fit in and I felt that even if I stayed there ten years I still would not fit in. So I resigned the church, packed up my family and moved to Fort Worth, Texas, to work on a doctor-ate. I needed a job to provide for my three-year old daughter and new-born son, so I became a furniture salesman. Then my religious employee's health insurance went bankrupt, leaving me with thousands of dollars in medical bills. On top of that, I discovered that the furniture company for which I was working advertised in ways that conflicted with my personal ethics. I felt I could not keep the job. I attempted to find a ministry, but nothing opened up. I finally found another furniture sales position at J. C. Penney, which I knew to be a reputable company, but I had to settle for less income. I no lon-ger had funds to pursue doctoral studies. All the doors had closed.

During this period of time, I had many questions for God: "Lord, I thought you wanted me to get my doctorate and teach in a college. I stepped out in faith, believing you would provide. Why did you let this happen? Where are You in this? Why haven't you opened a door for min-istry? Is there something terribly wrong with me that You have benched me? You called me to ministry; how can I find fulfillment and purpose without ministry?"

That began a search for God's purposes for my life. It was sixteen years before I was able to complete a doctorate. Today, twenty-some years later, I am a university professor and administrator as well as an international seminar Bible teacher and author. I have found my niche, and continue to develop new dimensions and directions of that niche.

Maybe you have not been able to find your niche. You are wondering what God's will and purposes are for your life. You are uncertain if God has a call on your life. Finding the will of God often seems like a labyrinth—

a confusing, winding maze with detours and dead ends. Yet from God's perspective, there are no dead ends if we are seeking Him. I can assure you today that God has called you and He will fulfill His purposes for you. His Word encourages us, *"The plans I have for you [are] plans to prosper you and not harm you, plans to give you hope and a future"* (Jeremiah 29:11).

Paul exhorted, "understand what the will of the Lord is" (Ephesians 5:17, NASB). If we could not understand the will of the Lord, Paul would not have commanded it. You can know the will of the Lord. God has a plan for your life and it is a good plan. Our Heavenly Father has individual purposes for each of His children. No matter how difficult our circumstances may seem, God is able to turn it into something good for His intentions. David confidently declared that even in the midst of troubles and enemies, "The Lord will fulfill his purpose for me" (Psalm 138:8). Every member of the Body of Christ has an important function, even if it is not outwardly noticeable (Romans 12:3-6; 1 Corinthians 12:14-27). You can understand this—God has a place for you.

I want to share with you some of the keys God has revealed to me in finding His purposes for my life. I have found that they are universal principles rooted in Scripture for opening the doors of God's will. With the Apostle Paul, I encourage you, *"For I am confident of this very thing, that he who began a good work in you will perfect it until the day of Christ Jesus"* (Philippians 1:6, NASB). You can be confident that God has a purpose for your life and will fulfill His will concerning you.

Most of us have a key chain with all kinds of keys—house keys, car keys, office keys, elevator keys, and on and on. We fumble with the keys, trying to find the right one. Jesus said, "I have given you the keys to the kingdom of heaven." He has given us the keys. It is frustrating to fit a key in a lock only to find that it does not work in that lock. As a believer we have access to His keys, but many times we fumble with them, trying to find the right one. We just have to find out which key opens which door. While these are not all the keys to Kingdom Living, they are keys to finding your niche in God's kingdom. These keys can open a whole new vista of God's purposes for your life.

In the last book of C.S. Lewis' Chronicles of Narnia series, entitled *The Last Battle*, the children open the stable door thinking that they would be seeing the inside of the tiny, dark, smelly stable. Instead, it opened the door for a beautiful scene of green grass, open blue sky, fields of flowers, and groves of trees full of luscious fruit. They found that it was bigger inside than outside. When we open the doors of God's niche for our lives, it will be greater than we can imagine.

# Embrace God's Ultimate Purpose and Calling for Your Life

*"And we know that God causes all things to work together for good
to those who love God, to those who are called according to His
purpose. For those whom He foreknew, He also predestined
to become conformed to the image of His Son, so that He
would be the first-born among many brethren"*
(Romans 8:28-29, NASB).

## You Are Not a Grasshopper

Having grown up in a strict, legalistic holiness background, I had strong inner thoughts and feelings that I was a nobody. I felt unable to live up to the proper Christian life or please God. I was quite aware that without Christ I could do nothing, yet I had no comprehension of the other side of the coin, even though I knew the Scripture well: "I can do all things through him who gives me strength" (Philippians 4:13). Hence, I almost always felt like a failure because I believed I could do nothing. Even though I knew God called me to the ministry, I had spent several years struggling in ministry before I realized who I really was in Christ and what I could do through Christ.

God showed me the story of the Israelites failing to enter into the Promised Land (Numbers 13) as an example of their failing to understand who they were and what they had through their covenant with God. The land was beautiful and abundant, but they could not enter in because they viewed the inhabitants as giants, saying, "we became like grasshoppers in our own sight, and so we were in their sight" (Numbers 13:33, NASB). I too thought of myself as a grasshopper. The giants were just too big in my eyes, so I could not enter into my Promised Land, my niche. If we do not realize who we are and what we have in Christ, we cannot enter our Promised Land.

## JUST WHO DO YOU THINK YOU ARE?

I want to ask you a question: Just who do you think you are? You might be thinking, "Just who does he think he is, asking me such a question?" But hear me out. Proverbs 23:7 presents the principle: "As a man thinks in his heart, so is he." The Scripture is saying, "You are what you think." Commenting on this verse, A.W. Tozer affirmed, "To be right we must think right."[1] We may not know who we really are because what we think may not reflect who we really are intended to be.

The ancient philosopher Socrates recognized this universal truth when he proclaimed, "Know thyself." Do you know who you are? Knowing who you are is basic to finding fulfillment and your niche in life. If you don't know who you are, you can't know what your purpose is. Your purpose flows out of your identity. Many people go for years not knowing who they are, and so they are restless, going from job to job, place to place, experience to experience, in search of finding fulfillment, and ultimately of finding themselves.

We can only briefly touch on our identity in Christ in this book. I would recommend to you Neil Anderson's books on our identity in Christ: *Living Free in Christ* and *Victory over the Darkness*.[2] Anderson aptly observes, "It is not what we do that determines who we are. It is who we are that determines what we do."[3] He lists various Scriptures and confessions of faith of who we are in Christ. Recite these affirmations to yourself.

## I AM ACCEPTED IN CHRIST

| | |
|---|---|
| John 1:12 | I am God's child. |
| John 15:15 | I am Christ's friend. |
| Romans 5:1 | I have been justified. |
| 1 Corinthians 6:17 | I am united with the Lord and one with Him in Spirit. |
| 1 Corinthians 6:20 | I have been bought with a price; I belong to God. |
| 1 Corinthians 12:27 | I am a member of Christ's body. |
| Ephesians 1:1 | I am a saint. |
| Ephesians 1:5 | I have been adopted as God's child. |

| | |
|---|---|
| Ephesians 2:18 | I have direct access to God through the Holy Spirit. |
| Colossians 1:14 | I have been redeemed and forgiven of all of my sins. |
| Colossians 2:10 | I am complete in Christ |

## I Am Secure in Christ

| | |
|---|---|
| Romans 8: 1, 2 | I am free forever from condemnation. |
| Romans 8: 28 | I am assured that all things work together for good. |
| Romans 8:33, 34 | I am free from any condemning charges against me. |
| Romans 8:35 | I cannot be separated from the love of God. |
| 2 Corinthians 1:21 | I have been established, anointed, and sealed by God. |
| Colossians 3:3 | I am hidden with Christ in God. |
| Philippians 1:6 | I am confident that the good work God has begun in me will be perfected. |
| Philippians 3:20 | I am a citizen of heaven. |
| 2 Timothy 1:7 | I have not been given a spirit of fear but of power, love, and a sound mind. |
| Hebrews 4:16 | I can find grace and mercy in time of need. |
| 1 John 5:18 | I am born of God and the evil one cannot touch me. |

## I Am Significant in Christ

| | |
|---|---|
| Matthew 5:13, 14 | I am the salt and the light of the earth. |
| John 15:1, 5 | I am a branch of the true vine, a channel of His life. |
| John 15:16 | I have been chosen and appointed to bear fruit. |
| Acts 1:8 | I am a personal witness of Christ. |
| 1 Corinthians 3:16 | I am God's temple. |
| 2 Corinthians 5:17-20 | I am a minister of reconciliation. |

| Ephesians 2:6 | I am seated with Christ in the heavenly realm. |
| Ephesians 3:12 | I may approach God with freedom and confidence. |
| Philippians 4:13 | I can do all things through Christ who strengthens me. |

Taken from *Living Free in Christ* by Neil Anderson, © 1993, Regal Books [4]

If you are a believer in Jesus Christ, you can be assured that you are accepted, secure, and significant in Christ. Jesus declares that you are the salt and light of the world. God's purposes work out in a practical way how you can become salt and light in your own unique way.

If you know you are a child of God, you know that God desires the best for you. According to Romans 8:28, if you love Him, you are called according to His purpose. And if you are called according to His purpose, you can have confidence that God will cause all things to work together for good in your life.

My daughter's name is Sarah, which means "princess." Her name is fitting, for she is the child of a king! You are a child of a King too—a child of the King of Kings! When you realize that you really are God's child, then you can realize that in Christ you are a prince or a princess, a child of the King of Kings. You are royalty, or as Peter put it, we are a "royal priesthood" (1 Peter 2:9). You have both the inheritance and responsibilities of a royal child of God.

## GOD'S ULTIMATE PURPOSE—TO BE LIKE JESUS

What is God's ultimate purpose for our lives? It is not to preach or to evangelize; it is not to grow big churches and ministries, or even to be successful in our vocation or calling. All of these things are good, and may involve God's purposes. However, they are not God's *ultimate* purpose. Romans 8:29 declares that we are predestined to become conformed to the image of Christ. So God's ultimate purpose for each of our lives is to become like Christ, to manifest His character in and through our lives. There is no greater purpose. Every other purpose that God may have for us is subsumed in this purpose.

Therefore, according to Romans 8:28-29, everything that occurs in our lives is intended by God to make us more like Him and to draw us nearer to Him. To find God's purposes for our lives, we need to realize that God is more concerned about developing our character than developing our calling. Every pain, every delight, every disappointment, every joy, every failure, every success, every trial, every blessing is ultimately for the purpose of producing Christ-like character in our lives. Paul Billheimer puts it this way: "Every single incident, whether of joy or sorrow, bane or blessing, pain or pleasure, without exception is being used by God for the purpose of procuring the members of His Bridehood and maturing them in agape love."[5] – used or caused by God.² Important distinction.

## God's Ultimate Calling— To Reflect Christ through Our Lives

As we become like Christ, we find our ultimate calling by reflecting and radiating the light of Christ through our lives. Paul tells us of this great calling: "And we, who with unveiled faces reflect the Lord's glory, are being transformed into his likeness with ever-increasing glory, which comes from the Lord who is the Spirit" (2 Corinthians 3:18). When we are transformed in His likeness, others can see the love and presence of Christ within us. Luke records that when the people of Jerusalem "saw the courage of Peter and John, and realized that they were unschooled, ordinary men, they were astonished and they took note that these men had been with Jesus" (Acts 4:13).

When others see Jesus in us, their lives are impacted by our living testimony. As Francis of Assisi once said, "Proclaim the gospel always; if necessary, use words." Others are blessed and changed as we demonstrate the life of Christ through us, and we find purpose and fulfillment. God's ultimate calling is worked out in a myriad of ways in and through our lives—whether we are a pastor, a teacher, a chef, a football coach, a secretary, a laborer.

## God's Ultimate Desire—To Fellowship with Us

*"Here I am! I stand at the door and knock. If anyone hears my voice and opens the door, I will come in and eat with him, and he with me"*
(Revelation 3:20).

If we are believers in Jesus Christ, we all want to be used by God. This is natural and good, but that is not His ultimate desire for us. Ultimately, God wants to commune with us, to have intimate fellowship with us. Oswald Chambers writes, "The central thing about the kingdom of Jesus Christ is a personal relationship to Himself, not public usefulness to men."[6]

As I related earlier, I went through a period of time in which I was out of pastoral ministry for a year. Everything went wrong. I felt like I had been benched by the Lord. I felt as though I must be so low that the Lord could not use me. I had been gaining my fulfillment in life by being a pastor. I knew that I had been called to the ministry, so I felt my life was purposeless if I wasn't in full-time vocational ministry.

During that time, I came to realize that God did not intend my fulfillment in life to come from vocational ministry but rather from *Him*. The Lord was trying to get me to the place where I could accept that if I never pastored a church again, if I never was involved in full-time ministry again, I could still find satisfaction and peace in my relationship and fellowship with Christ. My "self-actualization" is found in Christ Himself, not in any vocation or calling. I did not understand it at the time, but God was showing me that He wanted what Oswald Chambers calls "Christ-realization."[7] He says, "I am not here to realize myself, but to know Jesus."[8] Yes, I receive great satisfaction in ministry, but my greatest satisfaction is in Christ Himself. An old hymn writer put it this way: "My goal is God Himself—not joy, nor peace, nor even blessing, but Himself, my God."[9] You cannot find your purpose outside of your personal walk with God and friendship and fellowship with Him.

While you are seeking an open door to find your niche, Jesus may be knocking at your door, wanting to fellowship with you.

## OUR SUPREME AMBITION—TO PLEASE CHRIST

*"So we make it our goal to please him . . ."* (2 Corinthians 5:9).

We have many ambitions, but the one that should be above all else is the ambition to please Christ. When I fell in love with my wife, I wanted to do everything I could to please her (and I still do!). It is not a duty, but a strong desire that motivates me, because I want to make her happy. In a similar way, when we really love Jesus, we want to make Him happy, and that motivates us to do whatever we can to please Him. Oswald Chambers writes that our chief goal should not be "ambitious to win souls or establish churches or have revivals, but being ambitious only to be 'accepted of Him.' . . . Any ambition which is in the tiniest degree away from this central one of being 'approved unto God' may end in our being castaways. Learn to discern where the ambition leads."[10] Again Chambers writes, "My worth to God in public is what I am in private. Is my master ambition to please Him and be acceptable to Him, or is it something else, no matter how noble?"[11]

The important thing to understand about pleasing Christ is that *He* is the one who makes it possible for us to please Him. I had to learn

— *18* —

that instead of *trying* to please Christ, I needed to realize that on the one hand, I cannot do it without him, but on the other, if I focus my attention on Him, He enables me to do it. We work out our salvation with fear and trembling, for it is He who is at work within us (Philippians 2:13).

## GOD'S ULTIMATE PURPOSE AND CALLING FOR YOU AND THE CHURCH

I once pastored a church in which I started a home group fellowship along with a couple who was attending our church. I had done marriage counseling with them and viewed this home group as an opportunity to be more involved in discipleship of their lives. I was leading a study using A.W. Tozer's classic book *The Pursuit of God*. A few weeks into the study, I got a letter from the couple saying that they no longer needed my services and that they would carry on the Bible study on their own apart from the church. They convinced most of the others in the group to cease attending our church and make this Bible study group their church. Tozer would have rolled over in his grave if he had known!

These were people who desperately needed to be part of a church body and actually needed ongoing discipleship and counseling, but they had their own ideas and felt they didn't need a pastor, even though they had little biblical training. I don't know what became of all the people in the group, but I know that some of them dropped out of church altogether. They felt that most churches, even the supposedly "free" churches were too traditional, or they had been hurt in their church experience and didn't want to be part of a church any longer. They believed they could just worship the Lord on their own and didn't want accountability.

Aside from the fact that the couple needed more counseling, they did not realize that their lives cannot fulfill God's will apart from being a part of a church, a local body of Christ. Clinton Arnold describes such a view of Christ and His Church as a decapitated Christ—"Jesus without a Body."[12] There is no such thing as being a "Lone Ranger Christian," just me and Jesus. Regardless of the reasons or bad experiences we may have had for becoming alienated from the Church, the author of Hebrews counsels, "Let us consider how to stimulate one another to love and good deeds, not forsaking our own assembling together" (10:25, NASB). Since we are commanded not to forsake assembling together, not to be actively involved in a Bible-believing church is an act of disobedience to God. God's purposes for our lives cannot be fulfilled without the church. Even if God has called

*[handwritten margin notes: What about isolated Christians on the field? Bruce Olsen? Is it impossible to serve as an isolated Christian or merely more difficult? Again, isolated believers in Vietnam? Missionary on the foreign field?]*

us to serve Him in a secular arena vocationally, it is through the church that we find our place, our roles, our gifts and callings, and find the spiritual nourishment and equipping to fulfill His purposes.

If you have been hurt by a church leader or church experiences of rejection, God does not intend for you to drop out of church altogether. If the church has failed to be the Body of Christ for you, you may need to find another local church. But then again, God may want you to stay and grow and help others to grow in that situation. Before you can go on in your walk with God and move forward in His purposes for your life, you need to forgive the people and churches who have hurt you. Resentments and unforgiveness become festering wounds that block you from fulfilling God's purposes for your life.

*Wise, good advice, but what about missions.*

## God's Ultimate Goal for You and the Church— To Grow Up to Unity and Maturity in Christ

*"It was he [Christ] who gave some to be apostles, some to be prophets, some to be evangelists, and some to be pastors and teachers, to prepare God's people for works of service, so that the body of Christ may be built up until we all reach unity in the faith and in the knowledge of the Son of God and become mature, attaining to the whole measure of the fullness of Christ.*

*Then we will no longer be infants, tossed back and forth by the waves, and blown here and there by every wind of teaching and by the cunning and craftiness of men in the deceitful scheming. Instead, speaking the truth in love, we will in all things grow up into him who is the Head, that is, Christ. From him the whole body, joined and held together by every supporting ligament, grows and builds itself up in love, as each part does its work"* (Ephesians 4:11-16).

God's purpose for our individual lives is bound up in the purpose of the Church. There is no way we can fulfill God's purpose for our lives without the Church. Contrary to the beliefs and practices of hermitic monks, we cannot become holy and Christ-like without the Church. We need one another in the Body of Christ. The Church is incomplete and unfulfilled without you and me; we are incomplete and unfulfilled without the Church. My brothers and sisters in the Lord contribute to my spiritual growth. And God intends that the Church come to maturity through everyone (yourself and myself included) doing their part. If we are not

*Even missionaries need a home church.*

joined and held together with the rest of Christ's Body, we cannot grow, we cannot be built up, and we cannot fulfill God's work for us.

In the book *Christian Healing* by Mark Pearson, his wife, an osteopathic physician, describes our need for the church to bring completeness, fulfillment, and healing to our lives, using the picture of a rock tumbler: "The abrasion of the sand and the constant friction of the other stones rubbed away the rough spots on the stones and eventually polished them to a finish almost like glass. So community life is with us. If we avoid our troubles (the sand) or the pressures of other personalities (the other stones), we may be more comfortable but we will be incomplete. . . . In our search for wellness and health we must sometimes accept discomfort."[13]

## GOD'S ULTIMATE CALLING FOR YOU AND THE CHURCH— TO MAKE DISCIPLES

*"Then Jesus came to them and said, 'All authority in heaven and on earth has been given to me. Therefore go and make disciples of all nations, baptizing them in the name of the Father and of the Son and of the Holy Spirit, and teaching them to obey everything I have commanded you. And surely I am with you always, to the very end of the age.'"* (Matthew 28:18-20).

*[handwritten margin note: → compare with Mark 16:15-18, Discipleship vs. preach the gospel? → a bit of both perhaps?]*

The Great Commission from Jesus to the Church is not to evangelize the world, but to make disciples. There is no effective evangelism without discipleship. The ultimate call of the Church is disciple-making.

*[handwritten margin note: What about Mark 16?]*

Your calling is bound up in the church's calling. Since the church is called to make disciples, and you are a part of the Church, no matter what your occupation or vocation, you are called to make disciples. To make disciples, you first of all need to be a disciple. It is sad to see how many church leaders don't know how to make disciples because they have never been discipled themselves.

*[handwritten margin note: There is no discipleship w/out evangelism]*

The Greek word for disciple is *mathetes*, from which we get our English words mathematics and methodical. The idea of discipleship is order and structure in our lives. The root verb from which this word comes is *meno*, translated "to abide," from which our English word "remain" is derived. The word "mentor" also comes from this root. The core idea is to remain with, to persist, to persevere, to keep in order. We cannot be a disciple if we are not remaining with other disciples and if we are not persevering in being discipled. If you have not been discipled, find a mature Christian to mentor you.

*[handwritten note: → Do my parents count? ☺]*

Regardless of your vocation, God's calling for your life is to be a disciple-maker. Every believer can be a disciple-maker, one who shows the way to following Jesus. Luke records that even Saul, as a new convert, had his own disciples (see Acts 9:25, NASB). They were people saved through his preaching, as well as probably those who were converted along with him on the Damascus road. Therefore, no matter how young a Christian you are, you can lead a person as far as you yourself have gone. You can mentor a person in the skills you have achieved and the wisdom you have acquired.

How God's purpose for you to be a disciple-maker is worked out in your life will be determined by the additional keys to finding your purpose and calling described in future chapters.

## GOD'S ULTIMATE DESIRE FOR YOU AND THE CHURCH— INTIMATE COMMUNION WITH HIS BRIDE

*"Christ also loved the church and gave Himself up for her; that He might sanctify her, having cleansed her by the washing of water with the word, that He might present to Himself the church in all her glory, having no spot or wrinkle or any such thing; but that she should be holy and blameless."* (Ephesians 5:25-27, NASB).

Just as God's ultimate desire is to have fellowship with us each individually, so His ultimate desire for the Church is to be united in intimate communion with the Church—His Body, His Bride. He wants to abide with us and wants us to abide with Him through His Church. We will never find our ultimate purpose and calling if we are not in active fellowship, worship and service with a local church. We will never find our ultimate purpose and calling if we are not building up the Body of Christ and contributing to the unifying and maturing of the Church.

*Again, what about*

*Bruce Olsen.? Or Isaiah for that matter.? Elijah.?*

*- Not rejecting this, just thinking that we can get direction from God wherever we are, even locked in an Iranian prison.*

## FOR FURTHER REFLECTION

1. Do you know who you are in Christ? Who are you?

2. In what ways have you fulfilled God's ultimate purpose for your life?

3. In what ways have you not fulfilled God's ultimate purpose for your life? What steps do you need to take to be in God's ultimate purpose for you?

4. How strong is your relationship and fellowship with Jesus Christ? What do you need to do to improve that relationship and grow closer to Him?

5. Is the chief goal of your life to accomplish something great, or to please God?

6. Are you actively plugged into a good Bible-believing church?

    a. If so, are you growing from relationship and fellowship with others?

    b. If you are not active in a church, why not? Do you realize what you are missing?

7. If you have been hurt by people or experiences at church, have you forgiven those who hurt you?

8. Are you finding your purpose and calling in and through your church?

———◆·◆———

# Become Equipped to Minister

*"to prepare God's people for works of service, so that the body of
Christ may be built up"* (Ephesians 4:12).

An old gospel hymn proclaims:

*"Ready to go, ready to stay, ready my place to fill;
Ready for service, lowly or great, ready to do His will."*[14]

A re you ready for God's purposes for your life? Although God
sometimes calls us before He equips us, nonetheless we need to be
equipped for God's purposes before we can fulfill His purposes. If you
are struggling to find God's purpose for your life, it may be that you are
not yet adequately prepared to carry out His desire. You may say, "I am
ready; I am prepared." But is it the right preparation for the particular
purpose God has in mind for you at this particular time?

Every believer is called to be a minister. That does not mean that
you must go into a full-time Christian vocation, but rather that you are a
minister—a servant—of Jesus Christ wherever you are, in whatever state
of life, in whatever occupation. If you are called, you need to be prepared
for the task to which God has called you.

Some people think that if they are called, they can just go forth and do
it. In some rare cases, God has given an instantaneous, powerful anointing
that enables a person to minister with power, authority and effectiveness,
but that is not God's usual path. Yes, God launched a newly converted teenage boy by the name of Charles Spurgeon into worldwide ministry and
popularity, but his heart had been prepared throughout his childhood.

Dwight Moody, Smith Wigglesworth, and A.W. Tozer, all without formal high school education, were used greatly by God. Yet each in his own way was specially prepared by God in the seminary of life.

Also remember that God spent 80 years preparing Moses for 40 years of wilderness ministry. The Apostle Paul, trained as a rabbi, had to undergo wilderness training, and though called at conversion to be an apostle to the Gentiles, did not achieve that status until 14-17 years later. Even Jesus was prepared 30 years for only 3 ½ years of earthly ministry.

Your call may or may not be to full-time vocational church or parachurch ministry. But you are called by God nonetheless. And that calling is no less valuable to God than someone with a full-time ministry. You may be called by God to fulfill your calling as an engineer, as a computer programmer, as a retail sales clerk, even as a ditch digger.

Even if God is calling you to full-time ministry, He may have an unusual process of preparation. One of my mentors, Dr. Charles Farah, received his Ph.D. from the University of Edinburgh and joined the Navigators organization. One of his first tasks after he joined the staff was to help prepare a grave for the newly-deceased founder of the Navigators, Dawson Trotman. Even with a Ph.D., he was called to be a servant.

For a period of about five years I served as a bi-vocational pastor, working full-time for J.C. Penney selling jewelry. I had a hard time accepting that it was God's will for me, having a Masters degree in Theology with Honors, to be selling jewelry. But God was not only humbling me, He was also using me. I had numerous opportunities to witness, counsel and pray with people that I would not have had otherwise. Some of the people ended up attending my church! All of our experiences of life are intended by God to prepare us to fulfill His purposes for us effectively.

The Scripture describes at least ten areas of equipping for ministry. This is a brief overview of those ten areas. I hope to devote another book describing in greater depth these essential arenas for equipping. Even if your ministry is not a full-time calling vocationally, you can become equipped in these ten areas, and be used by God to minister to others.

## BECOME EQUIPPED IN RESTORATION

As a young pastor, I suffered periods of severe chronic depression related to some past issues in my life, particularly in the areas of perfectionism, legalism, and poor self-image. My past and my depression negatively affected my attitude and the way I preached as well as my effectiveness in ministry. I was trying to bring healing and restoration to others without becoming healed myself. And in so doing, I wounded others. It was only as I went through therapy with a Christian counselor that I was gradually healed of those wounds. Then my preaching and pastoral care became more positive, empathetic, and effective.

If you are wounded or hurt, in order to find God's purposes for your life, whether in secular work or in a ministry vocation you need to be healed, to be restored in His image. Spiritual or emotional dysfunctionalism hinders you from becoming all God wants you to be and from doing all God wants you to do. Paul tells us in 2 Corinthians 1:3-7 that God comforts us in our affliction that we may comfort others. So many people cannot fulfill their God-given potential because of generational bondages, unhealed wounds, bitterness, or unforgiveness from their past. We must be careful not to be bleeding on others because of our wounds.

According to 2 Corinthians 5:17-20, God has given us a ministry of reconciliation. As we have been reconciled to God, so we can become agents of reconciliation for others. Henri Nouwen writes that we are "wounded healers." God can use us even if we are not totally healed as long as we are not bleeding on others or causing others to be wounded. For example, Charles Spurgeon had a remarkable healing ministry in which thousands of people were healed, yet he suffered from illnesses without receiving healing himself. In fact, he went through months of depression, sometimes psychologically and physically incapacitated, yet God used him greatly even in his weaknesses.

While God does often use us in spite of our issues, some people never find their niche because of unresolved issues in their lives. Doors slam shut because of unhealed wounds. Is there some area of your life that needs to be restored—physically, emotionally, spiritually—in order to be effective in fulfilling God's purposes for you?

## BECOME EQUIPPED IN FAITH

The author of Hebrews exhorts us, "Without faith it is impossible to please God" (11:6). In order to fulfill God's purposes in our lives and find our niche, we must learn to walk in faith. Paul wrote the fledgling Thessalonian church that he desired to return to them in order to "complete [Greek, katartizo—equip] what is lacking in your faith" (1 Thessalonians 3:10, NASB).

I had been in ministry several years before I realized how I was lacking in faith. As I mentioned in Chapter 1, the Lord showed me from the story of the Israelites failing to enter the Promised Land that I was like them, viewing myself as a grasshopper and everyone and everything else as giants. God revealed to me that there is a correlation between low self-image and lack of faith. My poor self-image prevented me from having a strong faith. If we don't know who we are, we cannot exercise faith, confidence in God's working through our lives. Lack of faith keeps us from being successful at what God calls us to do in life.

Our faith must be both strong and sound. Some emphasize becoming strong in faith, but their teachings and practices of faith are not always sound. Others stress becoming sound in faith, but are often so critical of the perceived weaknesses and errors of those who are bold in their faith that they leave a person wondering whether there can be any kind of strong faith. My earlier book, *Moving Mountains: Lessons in Bold Faith from Great Evangelical Leaders*, provides a path that enables believers to exercise a faith that is both strong and sound.[15]

Is your faith both bold and confident, on one hand, and healthy in doctrine and practice, on the other? What is lacking in *your* faith? You can pray, "Lord, I believe; help me in my unbelief." Use the little faith you have, and God will add to it. Faith grows through exercise. A confident and healthy faith will enable you to fulfill God's purposes for your life successfully.

## BECOME EQUIPPED IN THE WORD

How well do you know the Scriptures? You can come to know God's will by knowing God's Word. Jesus proclaimed, "The words that I have spoken to you are spirit and are life" (John 6:63, NASB). The Scriptures are life and can bring life to you, helping you to find your niche. George Müller became a great man of faith used mightily by God in both business and ministry. What was the secret to his power? He became saturated with the Word of God, reading through the Bible yearly, even as many as four times in one year, and memorizing large portions of Scripture. As a result, God gave him purpose and direction, wisdom, and business acumen to build and operate several orphanages by faith alone.

It is not enough to know the Word; we also need to know how to interpret and apply the Word properly. Some people use the open-and-point method of guidance, claiming a Scripture verse as a promise for themselves without regard to the context or what it originally was intended to mean. Many people cannot find their purpose because they are misunderstanding or misapplying the Scripture.

Finally, we need to know how to share the Word. Peter writes: "Always be prepared to give an answer to everyone who asks you to give the reason for the hope that you have" (1 Peter 3:15). If you don't know how to share the Word of God with others or to give an appropriate answer for the hope God has put within you wherever you are, you are missing God's purpose for your life. God places you in a job or vocation or situation for the purpose of sharing the Good News of Jesus Christ with others.

In what ways are you equipped in the Word of God? How can God's purposes be fulfilled through the Word of God in your life? In what ways do you need to be equipped in the Word?

## BECOME EQUIPPED IN THE SPIRIT

As a college freshman, I had a heart for the Lord and a desire to bring people to Christ. I even went on an evangelistic ministry team from my Christian college to Daytona Beach, Florida, during spring break in 1970. Although I shared my faith with other college students hanging out on the beaches, I was frustrated and felt like I was ineffective.

Just a few weeks later, a college ministry team from the Asbury College revival that had recently broken out on campus visited the church where I was attending. They gave glowing testimony of the moving and power of the Holy Spirit upon them and lifted their arms high toward heaven in worship and praise of God. Even though I had felt I was filled with the Spirit, I realized I was missing something they had—the overwhelming power of the Spirit. I began to seek the Lord, and one night knelt and asked the Lord to fill me to overflowing. The power of God came upon me and I wept and praised God. I went from there in the power of the Spirit such as I had never experienced before. I began to share my faith with boldness and was inspired to launch a youth ministry that grew rapidly. I began to have an insatiable hunger for prayer, intercession and the Word of God, and my ministry increased even more.

Although Jesus had sent out the Twelve, and later the Seventy, to minister before His death, after His resurrection, He did not automatically send them out again. Rather, Jesus told His disciples, "Wait in Jerusalem until you are clothed with power from on High." Have you been endued with power from on high? Do you have that power in your life? If you are a believer, you received the indwelling Holy Spirit when you were born again. You have the Holy Spirit within you. But has the power of the Spirit been released from your life? In John 7:38, Jesus said, "From his innermost being shall flow rivers of living water" (NASB). Are the rivers of living water flowing out of your life?

Whatever you want to call it—the baptism in the Spirit, the filling of the Spirit, the second blessing, a crisis experience of the Spirit—God wants to empower you with His Spirit, releasing His Spirit's power from deep within you. You have that reservoir of the power of the Spirit waiting to be released, not in trickles, but in rivers of living water. That power will enable you to find God's niche for you and to perform your job or vocation more capably beyond your own natural capacity.

Before Jesus ascended, He told His disciples, "When the Holy Spirit comes upon you, you shall receive power, and you shall be My witnesses in Jerusalem, Judea, Samaria and the uttermost parts of the earth. Jesus wants to equip us with His power through the Holy Spirit. The chief purpose of that empowering is to be His witnesses. Have you received that empowering to witness? Is it evident in your life?

As a Christian you have been given authority of the believer to overcome sin, temptation and the Evil One. However, just as a police officer may need backup power to reinforce His authority, so as believers we need to have extra power to overcome the attacks of the Enemy. Using an analogy from physics, it is the difference between potential energy, or energy at rest, and kinetic energy, or energy in action. We all have potential energy from the Holy Spirit, but that energy has not always been released, put into action. The power to be a witness of Jesus is manifested in three ways:

- Power to *speak* a witness—boldly, confidently, with wisdom, spontaneity, and the leading of the Holy Spirit (sometimes known as proclamation evangelism) in whatever situation.
- Power to *live* a witness—through holy living, victory over sin and temptation and Christ-like character wherever you are (lifestyle evangelism)
- Power to *demonstrate* a witness supernaturally—through demonstrations of God's power such as healing, miracles, speaking in tongues, manifestations or revelations from the Lord (power evangelism)

Evangelical Christians emphasize the power to speak a witness; holiness churches stress the power to live a witness; charismatic and Pentecostal churches call attention to the power to demonstrate a witness supernaturally. All three types of spiritual power are vital to Christian living. However, the prime key from which the others flow is the power to *live* a witness. If a person speaks powerfully with great wisdom and anointing from the Holy Spirit, but does not show God's power by Christ-like living, that witness is nullified. If a person speaks with the tongues of men and of angels, or has great faith, or supernatural knowledge, but lacks Christ-like love and the fruit of the Spirit, he is as a noisy gong or clanging cymbal.

Do you have that power actively operating in your life? Is it being released and expressed in all three dimensions? Are you developing and stirring up the spiritual gifts God has given you? Have you learned to walk in the Spirit and be led by the Spirit?

## BECOME EQUIPPED IN CHARACTER

The most important area of equipping in order to find our niche is character-building. As mentioned earlier, God is more interested in our character than He is in our ministry. God has purposes for us, but those purposes cannot be fulfilled without godly character qualities. He has vessels of honor and vessels of dishonor. He would rather use us as a vessel of honor. Paul exhorts, "Discipline yourself for the purpose of godliness" (1 Timothy 4:7, NASB). The Greek word for "discipline" is *gymnazo*, from which we get our English words "gymnastic" and "gymnasium." God wants us to have a spiritual workout to become spiritually fit. Paul furthered instructed Timothy, "Therefore, if a man cleanses himself from these things, he will be a vessel for honor, sanctified, useful to the Master, prepared for every good work" (2 Timothy 2:21, NASB).

Character is most often forged in the flames of trial. If you want to be used by God, you must go through the fire. To use another analogy, if we will not be pliable in God's hands, he may have to break us and remold us. The painful experiences of our lives are intended by God to make us more like Christ.

God wants to make a beautiful diamond out of our lives. Do you know where diamonds come from? They come from coal. And where does coal come from? It comes from dead, decaying plants. Something has to die. How do dead, decaying plants become coal? By time and heat and pressure, and more time and heat and pressure, and *more* time and heat and pressure. And what do you have? Diamonds? No—you've got coal! Now we understand that God can use coal. Coal can provide heat and comfort. But coal is dirty and smelly and messy.

God would rather use us as diamonds. So how does He make us into diamonds? By still *more* time and heat and pressure, and *more* time and heat and pressure, and *more* time and heat and pressure. And *then* we become diamonds!—but God is not done with us yet, because we are still diamonds in the rough. He still needs to do a lot of cutting to bring out the facets of our character to reflect His brilliance.

In what ways has God shaped your character to fulfill His purposes and open doors for your life? In what areas do you need to become more equipped in character?

## BECOME EQUIPPED IN PRAYER

We find our niche and God's purposes only through our prayer life with God. Yet praying does not always come naturally. The disciples asked Jesus, "Lord, teach us to pray." We need to be trained in prayer. Jesus responded, "Pray in this manner," giving them a format or outline of how to pray.

Does your prayer life ever seem flat? Perhaps it is because your prayers are two-dimensional. A picture of the Rocky Mountains is beautiful, but it is nothing like being there, because it is only two-dimensional. It lacks depth. I have discovered that to be equipped to pray effectively and understand God's purposes we need a three-dimensional prayer life.

• First, we need daily, devotional prayer. We need to have a set-aside time—an appointment with God—every day.

• Secondly, we need the spirit of prayer. Paul exhorted the Thessalonian church, "pray without ceasing." This means maintaining an attitude or spirit of prayer throughout the day. This atmosphere of prayer is what Brother Lawrence called "practicing the presence of God."

• Thirdly, we need times of extended fervent prayer. James wrote, "The effectual fervent prayer of a righteous man availeth much" (James 5:16, KJV). Spurgeon declared, "He who prays without fervency does not pray at all."[16] The Greek word for fervent is related to our English word "energetic." Our prayers need to be energetic, not anemic.

The first two dimensions involve our worship and communion with God. The third involves petition, intercession and spiritual warfare. Petition or intercession without communion will only be prayers hitting the ceiling. Warfare without worship will result in attack and defeat. Without daily devotional prayer there is no consistency, stability or disciplined maturity. Without the spirit of prayer, there is no sense of God's continual abiding presence. Daily devotional prayer without practicing the presence of God is mere ritual—just going through the motions. Without fervent prayer, there is no depth, compassion or urgency. However, fervent prayer without daily devotional prayer is often undisciplined, impulsive, emotion and problem-centered. We need all three dimensions in balance. Is one of these dimensions of prayer missing from your life? Lack of one of these dimensions may hinder God's doors from being opened.

## BECOME EQUIPPED IN SPIRITUAL WARFARE

In order to fulfill God's purposes for our lives, we must realize that we are in a battle. Paul observed, "For a wide door for effective service has opened to me, and there are many adversaries" (1 Corinthians 16:9. NASB). The enemies of God, both human and satanic, will try to thwart us from finding our niche and accomplishing God's purposes for our lives. In fact, Paul admitted on one occasion that "Satan thwarted us" (1 Thessalonians 2:18, NASB). I carry around in my Bible a meaningful quote from J. Sidlow Baxter that I cut out of a church bulletin many years ago:

> There is an opportunity in every difficulty and a difficulty in every opportunity. That is why so many blessings are missed, so many heights left unscaled, so many fine chapters of service left unwritten. Some of the finest foreign missionaries are those who never went! They heard the call, they felt the urge, they were keen to go, they saw the open door and would have gone through; but there were adversaries, obstacles, discouragements; there was hesitation; the vision faded; and the grand vocation was never fulfilled.

This quote has helped me many times when I was ready to give up. Paul assured us, "For our struggle is not against flesh and blood, but against the rulers, against the powers, against the world-forces of this darkness, against the spiritual forces of wickedness in the heavenly places" (Ephesians 6:12).

As a believer in Jesus Christ you have been given spiritual authority. "To as many as received Him, to those who believe on His name, He gave authority to become the children of God" (John 1:12). Likewise, Jesus said, "I give you authority over all the power of the enemy" (Luke 10:19). Do you know your authority in Christ?

To be equipped in spiritual warfare, we must continually wear the full armor of God listed in Ephesians 6. If we are not wearing any part of the armor of God we leave ourselves vulnerable to the attacks of the Enemy. In addition to this armor, we need also to know how to use the weapons of praise, fasting, using the Name and Blood of Jesus, praying a hedge of thorns and protection, and binding and loosing. Are you equipped to use each of these spiritual pieces of equipment? What part of God's armor needs to be strengthened in your life?

## BECOME EQUIPPED IN DISCERNMENT

Accomplishing God's purposes for our lives, calls for discernment. A.W. Tozer has asserted that the greatest spiritual gift needed today is the gift of discernment.[17] Because of the deceptions and counterfeits of Satan, it is essential to be discerning of what is of God, of the flesh and of Satan. "But solid food is for the mature, who because of practice have their senses trained to discern good and evil." (Hebrews 5:14, NASB). Some areas for discernment include:

- Good from evil
- Nuances of good, better and best (As Oswald Chambers has said, the good can be the enemy of the best).[18]
- Accurately handling and interpreting the Word of God
- Flesh vs. Spirit
- True and counterfeit supernatural manifestations
- Flesh vs. demonic
- Psychic or soulish power vs. spiritual power
- Wise guidance and decision-making
- Immaturity vs. Impurity

Lack of discernment hinders us from effectively finding and operating in our niche. In what ways have you been equipped in spiritual discernment? In what ways do you lack discernment? How can you become more discerning?

## BECOME EQUIPPED IN CREATIVE SKILLS FOR HIS PURPOSES

Hebrews 13:21 is a prayer for God to "equip you in every good thing to do His will, working in us that which is pleasing in His sight" (NASB). The verb "to do" in Greek is *poeo*, related to the English word "poem," and means "to do creatively." The noun form of the same word is found in Ephesians 2:10, "For we are God's workmanship [Greek, *poema*], created in Christ Jesus to do good works." You are God's poem! God is a God of creativity, and he wants to work creatively in and through our lives to produce a variety of skills for His purposes.

How do you gain skills for your niche? One way is to hang around with those who are skilled in your area of interest, learning personally and informally from them by observing and listening. Jesus followed a four-fold pattern in equipping His disciples:

- **Jesus ministered and the disciples observed.** (John 1:35-43). Jesus said, "Come and see." "Come and follow Me."
- **The disciples assisted Jesus** (Luke 8:49-56).
- **The disciples ministered and Jesus observed** (Mark 6:35-44). Do you realize that Jesus did not feed the 5,000? I am not teaching a heresy here. Look at the text closely. When the disciples came to Jesus about the 5,000 plus people famished after being gathered for hours in the heat listening to His teaching, Jesus responded, "YOU feed them." Then he had them find the few loaves and fishes. All He did was to give thanks and break the loaves and fishes and give the twelve pieces to the disciples. Then THEY continued to break the food in pieces and distribute them to the thousands of people. The miracle took place in their hands.
- **Jesus sent the disciples out to minister on their own** (Luke 10:1-21). Then they reported back and were debriefed by Jesus.

You can do the same: watch someone else performing the skill, then assist the person, then do it yourself with others observing and evaluating. Finally, you can go out and do it on your own, coming back to discuss your experience with your leaders.

Once I took a young elder (some might call that an oxymoron!) with me to the hospital to visit the dying father of one of my church members. He was cantankerous and had been antagonistic to the gospel. The elder did not expect much to happen, but as I shared the gospel in a loving way to this man facing death, all his anger and animosity melted. He made his peace with God and became ready to meet Jesus Christ as his Savior and Lord. By observing and assisting me that day, the elder learned the power of God to change a seemingly hardened old man.

More formally, you can learn from a mentor or a coach, or you can pursue seminars and courses in your area of interest at a community college, Bible institute, college or university. Online and short-term modular courses are becoming excellent means to be trained in the creative skills God wants to develop in you. Many are finding second careers through pursuing fresh areas of study in colleges, graduate, and doctoral programs.

## BECOME EQUIPPED TO EQUIP OTHERS

Paul counseled Timothy, "The things which you have heard from me in the presence of many witnesses, entrust these to faithful men who will be able to teach others also" (2 Timothy 2:2, NASB). Spiritual maturity is not determined by how long we have been a Christian or by how many great spiritual experiences or revelations we have had. Rather, we demonstrate spiritual maturity by being a successful spiritual parent, not only by reproducing Christ's character within us, but by reproducing the life and character of Christ within others. It is not enough to become equipped in the areas above; God wants us to be prepared to pass on to others what we have learned and experienced spiritually, through the church, as well as in your job or vocation.

Any believer, no matter how young and inexperienced in the faith, can begin to disciple others. Acts 9 records that just after his conversion, Paul (then known as Saul) had disciples—probably those who were converted with him on the Damascus Road and those to whom he preached and testified on the streets of Damascus. You cannot take a person farther than you are, but you can take a person as far as you have gone. The more you grow, the more you can disciple others. God's purpose for your life may involve finding someone with whom you can share your skills, insights, knowledge and experiences. No matter what your vocation or area of expertise, you can be a mentor of others.

There are many kinds of mentors. The Big Brother/Big Sister program is a kind of mentoring. I was mentored by a publisher in the areas of writing and editing skills. My wife and I served as therapeutic foster parents for neglected and abused children for period of time. That was a mentoring/parenting role. Titus 2:3-5 speaks of mature women teaching younger women. When I have taught seminars on Ministry and Leadership Development and discipling, both men and women have often asked me, "Where can I find a man or a woman to mentor me?" There is a crying need for mentors.

These are ten areas in which every believer should become equipped for his or her niche. Some areas may be more useful for your niche than others, so concentrate on the areas you need most. At the same time, these ten areas are vital for every Christian. As you become equipped in these ten areas, you will become a more noble and usable vessel for God's purposes, no matter what your vocation. God will open up doors for you.

## FOR FURTHER REFLECTION

1. In what ways are you currently functioning as a minister of Christ by ministering to or serving others?

2. In which of these areas do you most need to become equipped?

3. What can you do to become equipped in these areas?

4. Are you being discipled or mentored by another mature Christian? If not, how can you begin? Think of some possible people who might mentor you.

5. Are you discipling or mentoring others? If not, who can you have an impact upon?

# Develop a Servant's Heart

*"Whoever wishes to become great among you shall be your servant;*
*and whoever wishes to be first among you shall be slave of all. For*
*even the Son of Man did not come to be served but to serve, and to*
*give His life a ransom for many"*
(Mark 10:43-45, NASB).

W hen I first started out in pastoral ministry, I must admit that I did not have a pastor's heart. I was a task-oriented person, not a people-oriented person. I was more interested in getting the job done and endeavoring to strengthen and stabilize the church ministry than in visiting and counseling people. I felt that ministry would be great if it wasn't for people!

A pastor's heart is a servant's heart, a desire to serve the needs of people. Biblical leadership is servant leadership. Through time, experience, and suffering, I developed a servant's heart. I began to care for people and view them through the eyes of Jesus. It transformed my attitudes, my patience and my ministry.

Developing a servant's heart is invaluable in finding God's purposes for your life. The Greek words for "minister" can also be translated "serve." To minister is to serve. If every believer is called to minister, then every believer is called to serve. The pathway to ministry and leadership is through serving. You will find your purposes and calling through serving.

There are seven characteristics of a servant's heart, described by the different Greek words for serving in the New Testament.

## 1. Waiting Eagerly and Alertly to Serve

One of the most common two Greek words in the New Testament for servant is *diakonos*. Our English words "deacon" and "diaconate" are derived from this term. It is translated variously as deacon, minister, or servant. Literally, it means "to kick up the dust by hastening, to run errands, what we sometimes call a "go-fer." The picture is of a runner bent low, poised to take off at the shot of the starting pistol and kicking up the dust.

The idea is that the servant is waiting eagerly and alertly to serve. Another analogy is that of a good waiter in a restaurant who is attentive to your needs, comes to see if there is anything he can do for you—bring some condiments, refill your drink, get you a dessert, etc. God can reveal His purposes for our lives and open doors of opportunity as we demonstrate an eagerness and alertness to serve in whatever capacity God may desire.

## 2. HUMBLING YOUR SELF

A second characteristic of a servant's heart is represented by the Greek term *latreia*, which means to serve by worshiping humbly or giving homage. A.W. Tozer is an example of one who loved God so much that he spent hours laying face down on the carpet in worship and prayer, humbling himself before the Lord.

The term *latreia* is related to our English word "latrine." Now that sounds exciting, doesn't it? The idea conveyed is to be willing to lower ourselves to do the most menial task, even to the extent of cleaning latrines. One of my mentors whom I mentioned earlier, Charles ("Chuck") Farah, is a model of this servant spirit. After receiving his Ph.D. from the University of Edinburgh in Scotland, one of the most prestigious universities in the world, he went to work for the Navigators. In the early days of his ministry there, this scholar actually did clean toilets. Not only that, but he also helped to dig the grave of Dawson Trotman, the founder of the Navigators. Some people jokingly call Ph.D.'s "post-hole diggers." He literally *was* a post-hole digger, but was not ashamed to humble himself for that that task.

If we will humble ourselves before the Lord to do whatever He asks, whatever is in front of us, he will exalt us and open up greater opportunities of service.

## 3. ATTENDING TO THE NEEDS AND WOUNDS OF OTHERS

A third trait of a servant's heart is expressed by the Greek word *therapon*, meaning one who attends to needs and heals wounds. Our English words "therapy" and "therapeutic" come from this root. The idea is one who is a healer, a nurse, a medical attendant. This word is used of Moses in Hebrews 3:5, "Moses was faithful in all His house [Israel] as a *servant*." The Israelites had been released from bondage by God through the servant's heart demonstrated by Moses. Moses attended to their needs, in spite of their continued psychological bondage to Egypt. He even acted as an advocate in behalf of them when God wanted to destroy the Israelites for their rebellion. He desired to heal their wounds and bring them into the Promised Land.

Dr. Robertson McQuilkin is a shining example of this servant spirit. As the president of Columbia International University, he had a broad and well-respected ministry. When his wife was diagnosed with Alzheimer's Disease he resigned his position as president of the university in order to care for his wife, who eventually did not even remember him.

Whenever we demonstrate a desire to bring healing to others and are willing to attend to the needs of others unselfishly we show this kind of a servant spirit.

## 4. HAVING NO RIGHTS OF YOUR OWN—BEING TOTALLY SUBSERVIENT

The Greek word used here in the New Testament is *doulos*. Some Nigerians once told me that in their culture an attendant is called a *doula*. Anthropologists use the term to designate a woman "experienced in childbirth who provides continuous physical, emotional, and informational support to the mother before, during and just after childbirth." A doula . . .

- Recognizes birth as a key life experience that the mother will remember all her life...
- Understands the physiology of birth and the emotional needs of a woman in labor...
- Assists the woman and her partner in preparing for and carrying out their plans for the birth...
- Stays by the side of the laboring woman throughout the entire labor...
- Provides emotional support, physical comfort measures, an objective viewpoint and assistance to the woman in getting the information she needs to make good decisions...
- Facilitates communication between the laboring woman, her partner and clinical care providers...
- Perceives her role as one who nurtures and protects the woman's memory of her birth experience.[19]

The term *doula* has also been used more broadly to mean household staff, or those who provide care for the disabled or elderly.

In the biblical concept, a *doulos* is a bondservant, the slave who has no rights of his own, the lowest of the low. This is the person who is completely subservient and obedient. It is the word Paul frequently uses to describe himself: "a bondservant of the Lord." This is the person who, in Oswald Chambers' words and example, is "abandoned to God."

A friend and mentor of mine, James Garrett, has written an excellent book entitled *The Doulos Principle: Called to Be God's Slaves*. He notes that the *doulos* principle contradicts contemporary values, opposes contemporary religion's emphasis on self, challenges the "Me Generation" mentality, and dethrones cleverness and guile.[20] He explains that "once a believer grasps the *Doulos* Principle he immediately has a new perspective on God and life. The *Doulos* Principle begins to mold his every thought and emotion."[21] He identifies several characteristics of a *doulos* attitude produced in the life of a believer who realizes he is a *doulos*: As God's *doulos*:

- *agape* love is the impelling force that motivates us.
- we express *agape* love through reverence and thanksgiving.
- we have an intense yearning to know our Master's will.
- we manifest an attitude of dependency toward our Master.
- we acknowledge that all of our talents and gifts come from our Master.
- we accept the experiences of life as God's training program.
- we practice the principle of planned neglect—avoiding all that would distract us from God's purposes.[22]

Some of the practical implications of being a *doulos*, Garrett writes, are that

*vocational*
- The Master ordains circumstances and results of the service of His *doulos*.
- The Master determines the *doulos'* sphere of service and chooses his ministry.
- The responsibility of the *doulos* is threefold (1) to accept that sphere of service, (2) to hear the Master's heart, concerning what we are to do in the sphere, (3) to commit ourselves to diligence and excellence within that sphere.
- Personal financial pursuits must not rule God's *doulos*.
- A *doulos* is content with his Master's provision.[23]

You see, finding our niche is not a matter of finding what we want, but a matter of finding God's niche for us as His bondservants. It is yielding totally to the will of God as in the classic hymn "I Surrender All." The universal sign of surrender is hands raised high in the air, holding onto nothing, hiding nothing.

As Christ's bondservants, we surrender to Him everything we have and everything we are and everything we desire. We live not for ourselves but for Him and Him alone. In the words of another old hymn, we pray, "Let my hands perform His bidding; let my feet run in His ways; let my eyes see Jesus only; let my lips speak forth His praise."

However, some may ask, "How do we reconcile the idea of the fact that we have been exalted in Christ as children of the King of Kings with being a *doulos* who has no rights?" Garrett explains, "A *doulos* has only those rights granted by His Master."[24] As His *doulos*, we only exercise our rights as the children of God as He sees fit. Oswald Chambers expresses it this way: "If you are living the life of faith you will exercise your right to waive your rights, and let God choose for you."[25] Yes, as Christians we can claim our inheritance in Christ, but we must always be willing to yield our rights for Christ's sake. Our niche is found in living for our Master, not for ourselves.

## 5. BEING WILLING TO SELF-SACRIFICE

The Greek word *leiturgeo*, from which we get our English word "liturgy," can be translated as "serve, minister, or worship," as in Acts 13:2. It has the meaning of volunteering willingly as a public servant and serving willingly at one's own expense. It is an act of self-sacrificial worship. It is a trait of a servant's heart to serve our Master without expectation of reward. We sacrifice our own wants and needs willingly because we love our Master and are willing to do anything for Him.

J. Hudson Taylor went through severe deprivations as a pioneer missionary to China, circumstances that we consider great sacrifices. Yet, amazingly, his attitude was, "I never made a sacrifice." For him, these things were not sacrifices, because he endured them out of love for God and a passion to serve Him whatever the cost.

When Billy Graham first started in ministry, he was shocked when someone gave him an honorarium. He wasn't expecting to be paid to preach the gospel; he just did what he was called to do. If we serve with an expectation that we deserve something from someone, we have lost the servant spirit.

## 6. BEING A HOUSEHOLD SERVANT—A SERVANT IN CHARGE

In biblical days an *oiketes* was a household servant, one who has become entrusted with the care of the home and family. The household servant has a closer relationship with the family than ordinary slaves. There is an intimacy, a bonding of trust and covenant love. The *oiketes* that has shown him or herself faithful and trustworthy in the little things, may become an *oikonomia,* a steward, a servant in charge. Because the stewards have proven themselves, they are granted responsibility and authority over the household to manage the affairs of the household.

Eliezar was a steward over Abraham's household, and would have inherited Abraham's fortune if Abraham did not have children. Many others in Scripture served their masters well and became servants in charge of their masters' work. Joshua, the servant of Moses, became the leader of Israel. Elisha, the servant of Elijah, inherited a double portion of his master's supernatural anointing in the Spirit. Timothy served Paul faithfully and was given apostolic authority.

If we develop an intimacy of relationship with our heavenly Father with the heart of an *oiketes,* He will promote us to a greater service and place of authority. He will say, "Well done, good and faithful servant, take charge of ten cities."

## 7. BECOMING A CHASTENED SERVANT OF A RULER

The final characteristic of a servant's heart is represented by the Greek term *pais.*

It is related to the word *paidion* meaning child, from which we get our English word "pediatrics." It is particularly used of the servant of a ruler, or a king's attendant. It is this word *pais* that is used of Jesus as the glorified Holy Child/Servant of His Father (Matthew 12:18; Acts 3:13, 26; 4:27, 30), and of David as a servant of the Lord (Luke 1:69; Acts 4:25). Not only is a *pais* a steward of a household, but is in charge of the ruler's affairs. It is both a humbled and an exalted position.

It is fascinating to realize that the root of this term comes from the verb *paio,* which means to strike or to beat. Another derivative is the word *paideia,* which means childhood training. The idea is the nurturing and the chastening or discipline of the children to grow to maturity. When Jesus is described as a *pais,* it indicates that he has been through the chastening process, chastised for our sins, and as a result has been exalted to the right hand of the Father. This does not mean that Jesus sinned, but that He suffered for our sins, and because He did so, He was glorified and raised to a position of authority. The author of Hebrews tells us of Jesus, "Although he was a son, he learned obedience from what he suffered, and once made perfect [mature], he became the source of salvation for all who obey him and was designated by God to be high priest in the order of Melchizedek" (Heb. 5:10).

So when we have been chastened, when we have matured through spiritual childhood training, we become fit to be exalted as an attendant of the King of kings.

I once heard Bob Mumford tell the story of a vision in which two young colts were romping around in a field. They were captured and put in a corral. One colt bucked the corral and escaped. The other colt stayed in the corral and embraced the regimen of being broken.

The scene changes to years later. The colt that broke free of the corral was now a thin, frail horse in a dry, brown field. He looked up and saw a king's carriage being led by horses on a road. He was amazed as he saw leading the king's carriage the colt that he had romped with years before, now a majestic, muscular, sleek stallion. He asked, "How did you come to lead the king's carriage?" The stallion replied, "Because I embraced the corral and let myself be broken, I was trained to carry the king."

When we allow ourselves to be disciplined by the King of Kings, we are exalted; He opens the doors; and we find our niche.

• Disciplined by God : allowing Him to correct wrong thinking, show us the error of our ways, convict us via the Holy Spirit. This does not mean sickness or negative circumstances, i.e. car accident.

## FOR FURTHER REFLECTION

1. How can you express a servant's heart with alertness and eagerness to serve?

2. In what ways can you humble yourself as a servant?

3. How can you attend to the needs of others?

4. What does it mean for you to be a bondservant, to waive your rights?

5. How can you serve sacrificially?

6. In what ways can you become a steward, a servant in charge?

7. How have you been chastened to mature you to become ready for a place of leadership?

# Minister to the Lord before Ministering for the Lord

*"While they were ministering to the Lord and fasting, the Holy Spirit said, 'Set apart for Me Barnabas and Saul for the work to which I have called them'" (Acts 13:2, NASB).*

Luke tells us that while the leadership team of the church at Antioch was *"ministering to the Lord,* the Holy Spirit *said,* 'Set apart for me Barnabas and Saul.'" It is in the context of ministering to the Lord that the Holy Spirit speaks and reveals the purposes of God. They were ministering to the Lord before they ministered for the Lord. What is ministering to the Lord? The Greek word here for "ministering" is *leitourgia* (from which the word "liturgy" is derived). It has the meaning of worship, as translated by the New International Version. Ministry to the Lord is worshiping the Lord. When we worship, God receives from us His worth.

We too need to minister to the Lord before we minister *for* the Lord. Richard Foster, in his classic book *Celebration of Discipline*, writes, "The divine priority is worship first, service second. . . . Service flows out of worship."[26] The Westminster Catechism says that the chief end of man is to enjoy God and glorify Him forever. Worship is enjoying the Presence of God. As David exhorted, "Delight yourself in the Lord and He shall give you the desires of your heart (Psalm 37:4).

## BE BEFORE DOING

You know the story of Mary and Martha in Luke 10:38-42. Mary sat at the feet of Jesus, listening to what He had to say. "But Martha," Luke tells us, "was distracted by all the preparations that had to be made." She asked Jesus, "Lord, do you care that my sister has left me to do the work by myself? Tell her to help me."

She did not get the response she expected. Instead, Jesus replied, "Martha, Martha, you are worried and upset about many things, but one thing is needed. Mary has chosen what is better, and it will not be taken away from her." The one thing that is needed, the thing that is better, is to be with Jesus, to be in His presence, to hear what He has to say.

I tend to be a Martha, wanting to be busy serving Jesus. Many times, especially in ministry, we become so busy serving Jesus, we miss Jesus Himself. We become frantic and frenetic, missing the peace of the Prince of Peace. So we need to be before we do.

It is not a matter of being instead of doing, but in being before doing. To be means to sit at the feet of Jesus, listening to His voice, basking in His presence. It does not mean laziness, idleness, or ignoring the needs of others. It means getting our signals and directions from Him before launching out in ministry.

When we are sitting still at the foot of Jesus, listening to His voice and gazing at his face, we are attentive to His needs and desires. If He wants anything, we can hear it in His tone of voice, in His facial expression, in a gesture. What if Martha, instead of assuming that all of this busy work needed to be done, sat at the feet of Jesus? Initially, she might be restless. She might feel guilty for not doing anything. She might sense an obsession to be up and doing. But if she remained at the feet of Jesus, His presence and voice would be calming and soothing to her, relieving her of her tension and pressure to perform. If he needed anything, He could just say, "Martha, please get me a drink of water." Or, "Martha, now it is time to prepare the meal." When we sit at the feet of Jesus daily, we realize His priorities and timing for all things. We realize what is important to Him.

## SEEK GOD'S FACE, NOT HIS HAND

We will not find the purposes of God if we keep anxiously looking for His purposes. As Oswald Chambers says, "If we are in communion with God and recognize that He is taking us into His purposes, we shall no longer try to find out what His purposes are."[27] I know of many couples who tried and tried to have children, but could not, so they adopted a child. Then suddenly they were able to conceive. When the pressure is off, the body is relaxed.

To use another illustration, in my senior year of college I became anxious that I had not found a woman to marry. I thought if I could not find one among all the beautiful young ladies on campus, where would I ever find one out in the world? However, when I eventually was able to surrender to God, I prayed, "Lord, I don't know how I am going to survive in the ministry without a wife, but I will trust you to take care of me. I am willing not to be married if that is Your will." When I came to that place of yieldedness, then God was able to prepare me for her to come into my life. Before I graduated from college, that relationship was blossoming and she was not even a student at the university I was attending!

In a similar way, if we keep searching for the will of God, rather than seeking God Himself, we will miss His will. David Henderson puts it this way, "If you pray to seek God's face, you'll know His hand. But if you're looking for His hand, you may miss His face."[28] Peter Nanfelt, former President of The Christian and Missionary Alliance, tells a story about a missionary who learned this lesson:

> When she was a child, this young woman was fascinated with stamps and coins from foreign lands. During her college years, she recalls that "God started using coins to speak loving truth into my life."
>
> She remembers one day in particular when she was outside jogging while wrestling with a decision. "What is best for me to do, Lord?" she pleaded. Right then, she glanced down to see a quarter in the road. She tucked it into her pocket. Lay that day, as she continued to cry out to God, He spoke clearly to hear, "Just as your eyes were fixed on running ahead and you found a coin, keep your eyes focused on Me. When the time comes to reveal My will and blessings, I will show them to you."[29]

If we keep our eyes on Jesus, He will guide us into His purposes for our lives.

## SEEK FIRST THE KINGDOM

When we seek first the kingdom of God and His righteousness, everything we need and everything God desires will be amply supplied (Matthew 6:33). Bob Buford comments, "God has always promoted win-win situations for His children. What is good for His kingdom is usually better for us as individuals."[30]

What does it mean to seek first God's kingdom and righteousness? It means, first of all, obedience to what we already know is the will of God. If we are not following through on what God has already instructed us to do, He will not reveal more of His will to us. Some people seek to go out and minister while neglecting their family, church or vocational responsibilities.

Second, it means centering our entire life around the kingdom of God. The Kingdom of God is God's reign, the Lordship of Jesus in our lives. If our life is centered around our family, our desires, our job, even our church, it is not centered around the kingdom of God. When we do center our life around God's kingdom and will, everything else will find its proper order and place. We will have sufficient time and attention for our family, our job, our leisure time, etc.

Third, related to this second point, seeking first the kingdom of God means discovering what the priorities of the kingdom of God are, and then reprioritizing our life accordingly. Ask ourselves the questions: What is most important to God? What will bring about the Lordship of Jesus? What will accomplish the righteousness of God?

✳ Take some time to seek God's presence, provision and priorities.

## MINISTER OUT OF THE OVERFLOW

One Sunday afternoon many years ago as a youth pastor, the Lord revealed to me this truth from His Word. I was sitting on the hillside behind the church, praying and meditating on Scripture. The Lord showed me from the story of the feeding of the 5,000 that ministry comes from the overflow of worship. As Jesus blessed and broke the loaves and the fish and gave them to His disciples, the food multiplied in their hands. They gave and they gave and they gave, but never ran out of food. In fact, after all the people had been served, each of the twelve disciples still had a basketful of food—one basket for each of them—more than they had started with. When we are in touch with Jesus, we have available to us a constant supply. We can give and give and give, and never give up, give out, or give in.

As a young man, my father was hunting with a friend in the mountains of Pennsylvania. As they were driving through the isolated mountains in my father's pickup truck, his friend noticed that the gas gauge was sitting on empty. He exclaimed to my father, "We are miles from the nearest service station, and we are going to run out of gas!" But my father just smiled and kept on driving and driving. His friend was amazed that the truck never sputtered to a stop. Then my father revealed to him his secret—he had an extra gas tank in the back of the pickup and had a full tank of gas!

If we are continually drinking in of the limitless reservoir of Holy Spirit, literally in the original Greek, "be being filled with the Spirit," (Ephesians 5:18), even though we are giving, we will never empty out. We will not burnout. We will not give up, give out, or give in. We suffer burnout because we have given of ourselves without continually receiving the nourishment we need and without continually being filled with the Holy Spirit. When we are in constant communion with Jesus, the ministry will become a natural overflow of that fellowship. God's purposes for our life will naturally stream out of that relationship.

## Abide in His Presence

Ministry out of the overflow of worship is accomplished by abiding in the Presence of God. If you want to know the purposes of God in your life, it is not enough just to get in the Presence of God, but you need to stay there as well. Jesus said, "Remain in me and I will remain in you. No branch can bear fruit by itself; it must remain in the vine. Neither can you bear fruit unless you remain in me" (John 15:4). A.W. Tozer declared that the Presence of God is more important than the program. It is more important to be with God and to abide in His presence than anything else you might do for Him.

"Be still and know that I am God," He beckons us (Psalm 46:10). A. B. Simpson writes of his own experience of this truth in a little article called "The Power of Stillness", written more than a century ago, yet still timely and timeless:

> Many years ago, a friend placed in my hand a little book which became one of the turning points of my life. It was called "True Peace." It was an old medieval message, and it had but one thought, and it was this—that God was waiting in the depths of my being to talk to me if I would only get still enough to hear His voice. I thought this would be a very easy matter, and so I began to get still.
>
> But I had no sooner commenced than a perfect pandemonium of voices reached my ears, a thousand clamoring notes from without and within, until I could hear nothing but their noise and din. Some of them were my own voice; some of them

were my own questions, some of them merely my own cares, some of them were my very prayers. Others were the suggestions of the tempter and the voices from the world's turmoil. Never before did there seem so many things to be done, to be said, to be thought; and in every direction I was pushed and pulled, and greeted with noisy acclamations and unspeakable unrest. It seemed necessary for me to listen to some of them, and to answer some of them; but God said, "Be still, and know that I am God."

Then came the conflict of thoughts for the morrow, and its duties and cares, but God said, "Be still." And as I listened, and slowly learned to obey, and shut my ears to every sound, I found after a while that when the others voices ceased, or I ceased to hear them, there was a still, small voice in the depths of my being that began to speak with an inexpressible tenderness, power, and comfort.

As I listened it became to me the voice of prayer, and the voice of wisdom and, the voice of duty and I did not need to think so hard, or pray so hard, or trust so hard, but that "still, small voice" in my heart was God's prayer in my secret soul, was God's answers to all my questions, was God's life and strength for soul and body, and became the substance of all knowledge, and all prayer, and all blessing; for it was the living GOD Himself as my life, and my all.[31]

How can we find God's niche for our lives? Perhaps we are looking for a vision, a voice from God, a prophetic word, or an angel. Sometimes God does reveal His purposes in those ways. However, it is not always, not even often through spectacular means. Elijah was a man who had a miraculous ministry, who operated in the supernatural. Yet when things were tough and he was seeking whether God had any purpose left for his life, it was not in a sensational way that God revealed Himself to Elijah:

For those
who see
God in every
natural disaster.
☺

＊ Then a great and powerful wind tore the mountains apart and shattered the rocks before the Lord, but the Lord was not in the wind. After the wind there was an earthquake, but the Lord was not in the earthquake. After the earthquake came a fire, but the Lord was not in the fire. And after the fire came a gentle whisper (1 Kings 19:11-12).

Where can the will and purpose of God be found? Not so much in the dramatic and the sensational, but in the quiet whispers of God's voice. Where is the stillness of God found? Where can we hear His "still, small voice?" We can only find it when we ourselves are still before God. When we cease striving, we can hear the voice of God.

So many people come to the entrance of the Holy of Holies of God's Presence and never enter in. Or they step in for a brief visit, but do not stay. God would have us to realize that the way to the Holy of Holies is constantly open and available, and that He desires us to remain in intimate communion with Him, not merely be His guest. In the Holy of Holies—abiding in His Presence—we will have no problem finding His niche for our lives.

## WAIT ON THE LORD

Psalm 37 has been meaningful to me during the trying times in my own life. Out of the trials of his life, David counsels three times in Psalm 37, "Do not fret":

- Do not fret when evil seems to triumph (verse 1).
- Do not fret when others are successful and you are not (verse 7).
- Do not fret when others do you wrong (verse 8).

Rather, he exhorts us, "Be still before the Lord and wait patiently for him" (verse 7).

To wait on the Lord does not mean to be passive and do nothing but twiddle our thumbs. It means to wait patiently, but expectantly. Psalm 37 gives us keys to waiting on the Lord.

First, David says, "Trust in the Lord and do good; dwell in the land and enjoy safe pasture" (verse 3). Trusting God means to go about our daily life with peace in our heart that God has everything under control and will take care of us. The second part of the verse means that we obey—we do good. We dwell in the land—that means we are settled, not restless. We enjoy safe pasture—the *New American Standard Bible* translates this phrase as "cultivate faithfulness." We do what we already know God wants us to do, and keep doing it faithfully, no matter what the cost, no matter how long, no matter if there seem to be no results. As the old hymn says, "Trust and obey."

Second, verse 4 tells us to "Delight yourself in the Lord." Be in an atmosphere of praise and worship. God cannot bless us or move in our lives if we are resentful, discouraged, or irritable. Seek the Lord for Himself, not for what we can get from him. Lamentations 3:25 counsels us,

"The Lord is good to those who wait for Him, to the person who seeks Him" (NASB).

Verse 5 says "Commit your way unto the Lord." This indicates that we must have a direction, that we are going somewhere. Our trials may have slowed us down or caused us to pause to catch our breath, but we are not paralyzed by our trials. We are in motion, but not in a frenzy. We take steps in faith, saying, "Lord, I commit my way to You. Guide me in Your direction. Direct my steps to follow you wherever you go. If I am not on the right track, show me, and change my direction." Verses 23 and 24 tell us that our steps are ordered by the Lord.

Verse 7 exhorts us to rest, or be still, and wait patiently. Psalm 46:10 literally says, "_cease striving_, and know that I am God." In a state of stillness without distractions we can hear the voice of the Lord. We can rest while we work and work while we rest. If we are frantic or frenetic, we cannot hear God's voice for all the noise around us. When we become still, we are no longer impatient, but at peace waiting on God. Paul Billheimer quoted an unknown source saying, "One of the severest tests of character is the ability to wait upon God without losing patience with Him."[32]

In verses 8-10 David reflects on the delay and what God is doing in the situation. As we wait on the Lord, it is a time of reflection on what the Lord is saying or doing during this time. Ask yourself: What is God trying to accomplish in and through my life at this time? Do I need to prepare the way of the Lord? What action do I need to take before the Lord can move? What do I need to change before the answer can come to pass or God's will is able to be done? Is there something I need to lay on the altar, to surrender to the Lord as my Isaac?

When we wait on the Lord, we will renew our strength and mount up on wings as eagles. We will run and not be weary, walk and not faint (Isaiah 40:31). Then we will be in a position to hear clearly from Him what He desires us to do or say, or where He wants us to go, and how He wants us to do it.

## FOR FURTHER REFLECTION

1. How is your devotional life? Have you been ministering to the Lord and delighting in Him, or have you just been praying to get answers? • Need to focus more time on ministering to Him.

2. Is there some area of your life that is not centered around seeking first the kingdom of God? How can you reprioritize your life around God's rule and reign?

3. Are you approaching burnout in your life? What might be the cause? How can you be renewed?

4. What keeps you from remaining in the abiding Presence of God? How can you deal with that obstacle in your life?

5. What do you need to wait on the Lord about?

   • Direction on where to live, work, attend Bible school, etc.; (relationships)

# Identify Your Dreams, Visions, and Burdens

*"Delight yourself in the Lord and He shall give you the desires of your heart. Commit your way to the Lord and He shall bring it to pass"* (Psalm 37:4-5).

*"Without a vision, the people perish"* (Proverbs 30:7, KJV).

Some people reverse this Scripture in Psalm 37, getting the proverbial cart before the horse by saying, "I am going to delight myself in the Lord so that I can get the desires of my heart." We don't go to God to see what we can get from Him. We need to seek to enjoy the Lord for *Himself.*

When we truly do delight in the Lord, He changes our desires into His desires. What we desire may not be what He desires, or our desires may be tinged with mixed motives. When we love and adore Him we want to do whatever pleases Him. He then gives us a yearning, a motivation, vision, a concern or burden. Amy Carmichael explains, "God has something much better for us than the thing we naturally desire. As we wait with all the desire of our mind fixed on Him, the thing we naturally long for becomes less pressing, the friction ceases, and we are set free to go on."[33]

Once one of my deacons came to me and complained, "Pastor, our church needs to do more evangelism." By that he implied that *I* needed to do more evangelism and preach more evangelistic sermons. I replied that I do the work of evangelism, but my gifting was as a pastor-teacher.

I came to realize, and eventually so did he, that God was putting that desire in *his* heart because that is what God wanted *him* to do. Eventually he became involved in missions, received training at a missionary school and is now a missionary pilot.

If you are saying, "Pastor, I think the church should . . . .", the Lord may be saying to you, "I want *YOU* to do _____." The Lord may have placed the idea, the vision, the desire in your heart because that is what He has in mind for *you* to do.

## WHAT THRILLS YOUR HEART?

Frederick Buechner has said, "The place where God calls you is the place where your deep gladness and the world's deep hunger meet."[34] If you have truly delighted in the Lord, He has likely have planted a desire in your heart. Ask yourself the questions: "What is it that thrills my heart? What is it that gives me passion? What is it that stirs and motivates me? What is it that gives me energy? That may be your niche.

In the classic movie *Chariots of Fire* Eric Liddell, the great Olympic runner, declared, "When I run I feel His pleasure." I can say that when I teach and preach and write and lead and mentor I feel God's pleasure. That is what He has called me to do. What is it you do that you sense the pleasure of God when you do it?

## IS THIS GOD'S DESIRE?

We need to check and make sure, however, that our desires are desires from God. Remember how David said to the prophet Nathan, "I have a beautiful palace, but our God Yahweh has only a tent. I want to build Him a grand temple out of my love for Him." It seemed like a good idea to Nathan, so without hesitation or forethought or prayer he replied, "The Lord is with you; go and build." But that very night God came to Nathan in a dream and told him that He had not called David to build the temple.[35]

So we need to seek the Lord to see if the desire is really from Him or from our own heart. A *good* thing may not be a *God* thing. George Müller asked four questions that provide a good model to ask yourself:

- **Is this desire *God's* work?**—Is this is something that you are sure God wants done, or is it your own idea?
- **Is this *my* work?**—Am I the person to do this task, to fulfill this vision? Is God calling *me* to do this?

- **Is this God's timing?**—Does God want this done now?
- **Is this God's way?**—Is this the way in which the God desires the vision to be fulfilled?

Sometimes it is not the vision that is wrong, but rather our interpretation of the vision is mistaken or inaccurate. A.B. Simpson had a vivid dream about lost Asians wringing their hands in anguish over their doom. He thus believed that God was calling him to be a missionary to China. But his wife Margaret did not see it that way, and she let him know. Was she a rebellious wife? Not at all. Rather, she helped him to interpret the dream, and gain the right focus. He never became a missionary, although he did eventually traverse the world in behalf of missions and founded one of the greatest missionary organizations in the world, The Christian and Missionary Alliance.

Likewise, Ruth Bell grew up on the mission field and believed God was calling her to be a missionary as well. When a budding young ministerial student proposed to her, she hesitated to say "yes," because it would not fulfill her vision for missions. When she accepted the proposal, she never knew then what God had in mind—a worldwide evangelistic ministry as the wife of Billy Graham!

## WHAT MAKES YOU CRY?

God's purposes for us may come as well in the form of a burden, a heavy concern for a need. Often times in the Old Testament, we read of "the oracle of the Lord." Some versions bring out the literal meaning, translating "the burden of the Lord." A burden is a concern you carry inside you, something that weighs you down, feeling that you need to do something about it. Ask yourself, "What is it that makes me cry? What is it that makes me restless, feeling that I cannot rest until I do something about it?" What is it that breaks my heart because it breaks God's heart?

Paul said, "Woe is me if I preach not the gospel" (1 Corinthians 9:16, KJV). Jeremiah cried, "His word is in my heart like a fire, a fire shut up in my bones. I am weary of holding it in; indeed I cannot" (Jeremiah 20:9). Not all compulsions are healthy, but this is a healthy compulsion.

This burden is not an oppressive state, but a strong urging or feeling of grief, sorrow, or anger over a situation, such as when Jesus was "troubled in spirit" (John 13:21). The New Testament Greek word for compassion is *splagchnizomai*, which in the old King James Version was translated "bowels of mercy." It means "to feel in the gut." Try pronouncing the word aloud: *"Splagchnizomai!"* Doesn't that sound like spilling your guts? It is that uncomfortable passion—compassion—feeling pain with—deep within your innermost being.

Sometimes people have asked me, "Pastor, could you visit so and so?" I have replied, "Yes, I can, but have YOU visited this person? If God has placed this person on your heart, maybe He wants you to go and see her. Others have said to me, "Pastor, I think this person needs help or needs counseling." I respond, "God has shown YOU that this person needs help so that you yourself can reach out to him with the love and care of Christ."

Have you ever had the experience of a certain person coming to your mind, prompting you to intercede for that person? God may be calling you to minister to that person, to make that person your project through prayer, encouragement, guidance, or help. There is an old chorus that expresses this prayerful attitude: "Lord, lay some soul upon my heart and love that soul through me; and may I humbly do my part to win that soul for Thee."

Sometimes God gives us a burden before a vision. When we become broken over things as they are, then He gives us a vision of what can be done or what can become. But we need not worry, because He will always provide what we need.

## Scout Out the Territory

When you believe God is giving you a vision or a burden, don't just sit on it. Investigate that need—do reconnaissance. Explore your options. Survey the possibilities. Scout out those that seem promising. Weigh the alternatives and choices. Spy out the territory like the Israelites spied out the Promised Land—to find out all we can about the particular thing God has placed on our heart.

I was sharing with a group of ministry interns about the experiences my wife and I had providing therapeutic foster care to neglected and abused children. A young woman came up to me during a break and exclaimed, "That's what I want to do!" Then she proceeded to ask more questions about therapeutic foster care and how to get involved. This is an example of searching out the burden or vision that God places within us. For instance, if God is giving you a burden for abused women or children, perhaps you can visit a shelter that cares for such people, talk with people who have been abused to see how they feel, what their needs are, how they can be helped.

Oswald Chambers writes, "When God gives a vision by His Spirit through His word of what He wants, and your mind and soul thrill to it, if you do not walk in the light of that vision, you will sink into servitude to a point of view which our Lord never had."[36] As God places it in your heart and mind, check it out, follow up on the leading in your heart.

## How to Make Your Dreams Come True

*Then the Lord answered me and said,*
*"Record the vision and inscribe it on tablets,*
*That the one who reads it may run"* (Habakkuk 2:2, NASB).

Someone has said, "A vision without a task makes a visionary. A task without a vision is drudgery. A vision with a task makes a missionary."[37] Someone else has quipped, "If we fail to plan, we plan to fail." Our dreams and visions seldom come about on their own by passively sitting back and waiting for God to do something. The author of Ecclesiastes wisely points out that "the dream comes through much effort" (Ecclesiastes 5:3, NASB). If God gives us a dream or vision, there are specific steps needed to implement that dream. When Joseph interpreted Pharaoh's dream, he gave Pharaoh a plan (Genesis 41:33-40). When Nehemiah asked King Artaxerxes for permission to rebuild Jerusalem, he gave the king a plan with definite times (Nehemiah 2:1-8). The prophet Habakkuk (chapter 2, verses 1-3) gives us a pattern for making our dreams come true.

### Step 1: Appraise the Situation

Habakkuk begins by saying,

"I will stand on my guard post
And station myself of the rampart;
And I will keep watch to see what He will speak to me,
And how I may reply when I am reproved." (verse 1, NASB).

We can see several principles of appraising our situation in this verse. First, Habakkuk says he will stand at the guard post. This means we should continue to stay at our watch, to stand on guard, being faithful to keep doing what God has called us to do at present.

Secondly, he says he will station himself on the rampart. That means we need to get to a high place to see far—to wait, meditate and gain perspective.

Third, he says he will keep watch to see. The Hebrew here means "to spy out, to observe everything carefully and diligently." Like the Israelites in the book of Numbers, we need to spy out the land before attempting to enter. We need to do research on the subject of our dream or vision, get the facts, and assess the need and our strengths and weaknesses before we more forward.

The phrase "what He will speak to me" can be translated literally, "what He will speak *in* me." Search your heart for what God wants to speak in you—what He wants to plant in your heart, what He wants to do in you to prepare you to fulfill His dream for you. We need to be open, receptive and teachable. Once we see what God wants to do in us, then we can reply to God's reproof, His work of testing and changing and honing us to get us ready for His purposes.

### Step 2: Define the Work

The second step is God's response to Habakkuk:

> "Record the vision and inscribe it on tablets,
> That the one who reads it may run" (verse 2, NASB).

Once we have been tested, refined and approved, then we can proceed with what God wants to accomplish through us. Through the assessing process, we gain clarity for the vision or dream God has given us. Then we need to "record the vision," write it down, describe it. You can start with random thoughts, brainstorming, or a list, then prescribe it, that is, give order and direction to it. When you write something down, you make it visible, concrete, specific and permanent. The phrase "inscribe it on tablets" in Hebrew literally means "dig out the sense and set it forth." It is an allusion to digging out cuneiform characters with a stylus on clay tablets. This means that we need to dig out the sense of the dream God has given us. It is a good idea to describe your vision in one sentence (and I don't mean a run-on sentence!), making every word count. Then further explain it in a paragraph or two.

In the verse above, God says to write down the vision so "that the one who reads it may run." In the context, it means tablets that were set up in the marketplace to announce something important, or of heralds, messengers, warriors, and horsemen who run to carry out a royal mandate. So we need to declare it, make it plain, explain it to others, to our family, friends, mature Christians, church leadership. As we share we solicit feedback, evaluation, direction and support. Then others can personally encounter and partake of the vision with us, and then run with that vision.

We need to always have our vision in front of us to remind and prod us to accomplish God's will and let nothing get in the way. God exhorted the people of Israel to keep reminders in front of them:

> And these words, which I am commanding you today, shall be on your heart; and you shall teach them diligently to your sons and shall talk of them when you sit in your house and when you walk by the way and when you lie down and when you rise up. And you shall bind them as a sign on your hand and they shall be as frontal on your forehead. And you shall write them on the doorposts of your house and on your gates (Deuteronomy 6:6-9, NASB).

I did something like this practice when I was a college student. I had dropped out of college for a couple of years to be involved in youth ministry, and when I returned to school, I was determined to do well in my studies with God's help. At the desk in my dormitory room I wrote several Scriptures on a card:

> "Study thyself approved a workman that needeth not to be ashamed" (2 Timothy 2:15, KJV).

> "Do you see a man skilled in his work? He will stand before kings; He will not stand before obscure men" (Proverbs 22:29, NASB).

> "The hand of the diligent will rule, but the slack hand will be put to forced labor" (Proverbs 12:24, NASB).

At the top of the card I wrote, "How badly do you want that 'A'?" Coupled with the understanding that the Holy Spirit is my ultimate Teacher, that motivation in front of me day and night enabled me to raise my grades from a "C" average to an "A" average in one semester. When we set something in front of us, it becomes a constant reminder and reinforces our focus and our resolve to carry on and carry through.

### Step 3: Develop Objectives

God further instructs Habakkuk: "For the vision is yet for the appointed time" (verse 3a). God has an appointed time for his vision for our life. As

Ecclesiastes 3:1 tells us, "There is an appointed time for everything. And there is a time for every event under heaven" (NASB). The Hebrew for "event" means "delight or desired pursuit." As we have said, He plants desires in our hearts, and wants us to pursue them for His sake. Our responsibility is to listen to the voice of God to discern His appointed times. And so, prayerfully, we set "faith goals," or objectives we believe God wants us to accomplish.

That means planning both long range and short range goals. We establish the ultimate long-term goal God desires for us, then we set short-term goals as steps toward the ultimate objective.

If, for instance, you have a goal to obtain a degree, whether a Bachelors, Masters, or Doctorate, there are steps to take to meet that goal. Say you believe God wants you to complete a Masters degree to serve Him in a greater way. You believe God wants you to accomplish this goal in three years. Determine how many courses a semester you need to take in order to complete the degree in three years. What courses should you take first, second, third, etc.? How are you going to finance it? How much money each semester?

What priorities do you need to set? How will you structure your time? What in your current life and schedule will you need to change?

### Step 4: Plan and Work Your Strategy

*"It hastens toward the goal, and it will not fail."* (verse 3b, NASB)

The Hebrew word for "hasten" means "to pant, to blow upon, excite, kindle a fire." We need to breathe life into the vision, to blow upon the sparks and kindle the flame. Vision must translate into specific strategies. Ask yourself and the Lord:

- What does the Lord want me to accomplish?
- Why does He want me to accomplish this vision?
- When does He want me to accomplish it?
- How do I implement this vision?
- What steps do I need to take and when do I need to accomplish each step? What is the sequence and what needs to be accomplished first?
- What resources do I need (facilities, equipment, supplies, arrangements, etc.)
- Who do I need to help accomplish this vision?
- Who needs to know about this and how do I communicate it?

- What training (knowledge, skills, credentials) is needed to accomplish this vision?

It is in this stage that you especially need to exercise time management. Paul counseled the Ephesians: "Therefore, be careful how you walk, not as unwise men, but as wise, making the most of your time, because the days are evil. So then do not be foolish, but understand what the will of the Lord is." (Ephesians 5:15-17, NASB). Here lies the importance of setting and reevaluating priorities.

## Step 5: Execute the Plan

*"Though it tarries, wait for it; For it will certainly come, it will not delay"* (verse 3c, NASB).

The Hebrew word for "wait" does not mean to just sit and twiddle your thumbs until something happens. Literally, it means to "to tie, bind, adhere to." It means to stick to it, to persist, to persevere. Don't let anything stop you. Don't let obstacles deter or derail you. Don't let people or circumstances dissuade you. Don't loiter or procrastinate. Don't get behind God. Don't give up. Don't lose hope. Be a doer of the Word, not a hearer only (James 1:22).

That may mean working the plan in stages or through different means than you had originally envisioned. God often works with us in creative and unusual ways to accomplish His purposes. As I mentioned earlier, I tried to work on a doctorate several times, but again and again the attempts failed. Yet I did not give up hope. I did surrender it to the Lord, but stayed alert to when and how He would make a way. When possibilities arose, I checked into them, and eventually a door opened.

Originally, I wanted to get a Ph.D. but finances and circumstances prevented it over and over. Then the opportunity emerged for me to work on a Doctor of Ministry degree with all tuition expenses paid. Even though it was a professional ministry degree, not an academic research degree like a Ph.D. that I wanted, the Lord opened the door and made the provision, so I took the step. Later, I was able to go on to complete a Doctor of Theology degree (equivalent to a Ph.D. in Theology) from a prestigious world-class university. Doing it God's way in God's timing and provision, I was able to complete two doctorates instead of one!

## Step 6: Review and Revise

Once you have gone through these steps, you may find need to revise your plans as the Lord gives you more insight and direction. Go back and reassess, rewrite the vision, establish revised objectives, rework your strategy, and continue to stick with it. Investigate apparent failings, and examine why you did not reach your goal. As you seek the Lord about the "why," He may show you that perhaps:

- It was not really God's goal after all.
- It was God's goal, but Satan interfered. If so, continue to persevere and overcome.
- It was God's goal, but man interfered. Then continue to persevere, and trust that God will turn it for good.
- It was God's goal, but you did not take the appropriate steps and sequence to accomplish the goal.
- It was God's goal, but not God's timing.
- It was generally or partially God's goal, but it was out of focus.

As you review and revise, let the peace of God rule your heart (Colossians 3:15).[38] To cite Robert Schuller, there is:

A goal you should be pursuing;

A dream you should be launching;

A plan you should be executing;

A project you should be starting;

A possibility you should be exploring;

An opportunity your should be grabbing;

An idea you should be working;

A problem you should be tackling;

A decision you should be making.[39]

## FOR FURTHER REFLECTION

1. What do you have a passion for? What thrills your heart? What gives you energy?

2. What do you have a burden for? What makes you restless? What makes you cry? What breaks your heart?

3. What are your dreams and visions? How can you know if they are from God?

4. How can you begin to implement your vision?

# Share Your Life Message

One of the greatest principles I learned from Bill Gothard and his Institute in Basic Youth Conflicts (now Institute in Basic Life Principles) is that God develops our ministry out of our life message. Your purpose in life often emerges out of the trials of life—your struggles, wounds, difficulties, failures, sorrows and losses—and how you have overcome, how you have been healed and restored, how you have gained victory over temptations or overwhelming odds. John Eldridge puts it this way: "Only when we enter our wound will we discover our true glory. As Bly says, 'Where a man's wound is, that is where his genius will be.' . . . it is out of your brokenness that you discover what you have to offer the community."[40] Paul declared that his sufferings were for the sake of others (Ephesians 3:13; Colossians 1:24). God saves us that we might become a blessing to others (Zechariah 8:13).

## Your Life Experiences Shape Your Life Message

Our experiences shape our future—especially our painful experiences. Either we can react to them negatively or we can respond to them positively. As Stephen Arterburn puts it, God wants to "transform your pain into purpose."[41] Let us consider a few who have transformed their pain into purpose:

- **Joni Erickson Tada** could have wallowed in self-pity after she became a quadriplegic, but found new purpose in God. Now she is renowned, not only by her artwork painted with a brush held by her lips, but by her testimony encouraging others to overcome their worst nightmares, tragedies and disabilities.

- **Lisa Beamer**, while expecting a child, lost her husband Todd who helped to thwart the hijackers on Flight 93 in the 9-11 terrorist attack. Now she shares a message of hope and courage.
- Baseball star **Dave Dravecky**, after losing his arm to cancer, found that life could have meaning after baseball. As the old saying goes, "If life gives you lemons, make lemonade."
- I had an opportunity several years ago to share the speaking platform at a college commencement with **Beth Nimmo**, the mother of Rachel Scott, the first student killed at the Columbine shooting. This was just a little over a year after the event, actually the anniversary of when Rachel would have graduated from high school. While still grieving the loss of her daughter, she was dedicating a scholarship fund to her daughter's memory. Out of the horror of the Columbine shooting, Rachel's parents have turned the tragedy into a message of sharing the gospel of Christ, and telling the heartwarming story in the book *Rachel's Tears: The Spiritual Journey of Columbine Martyr Rachel Scott.*

I was once teaching some of this material in a seminar on Ministry and Leadership Development in Chicago, and found out that the son of a woman in the class had been murdered just a week earlier. Yet in the midst of her grief, she was seeking to learn all she could about how she could minister for Christ. Through her grief, God was preparing her for her life message.

My son Chris spent the entire year of 1999 in pain with five hospitalizations and three surgeries. After months of painful medical tests—upper GIs, lower GIs, colonoscopies, and more—eventually he was diagnosed with the chronic debilitating illness called Crohn's disease. After consultations and medical treatments, the doctors finally decided to remove 18 inches of his intestines. We were told he would have to wear an ileostomy bag for elimination for four to six months, and that he would be in the hospital for up to a month and be out of school for three to four months—pretty rough for a 16-year-old. But God had other plans. Through his faith and determination and the prayers of hundreds of people, he remained in the hospital less than a week, returned to school in two weeks, and only had to wear the ileostomy bag for two months. Six weeks after his last surgery to reconnect his intestines (which took place two days before Thanksgiving), he was skiing on the slopes of Colorado with his youth group!

That experience, as excruciating as it was, has become part of my son's life message. Since that time, he has been in great health, has had a zest for life, and has been on fire for the Lord. The summer following his amazing rapid recovery, he went on a short-term mission trip to Guatemala. He had dreaded speaking in front of people, but he had opportunity to give his testimony of healing and renewed faith before a thousand people in Guatemala City square. Now he is studying for a master's degree in philosophy of religion. Forged through the fires of pain and life-threatening illness, Chris now finds purpose in thinking, studying, and writing about the meaning of life itself.

More recently, in 2007 I was diagnosed with rectal cancer. After seeking the Lord, I sensed Him directing me to use all of His spiritual, emotional, and medical healing arsenal—prayer, faith, confession of the Word of God, worship, Communion, abiding in Christ, positive mental attitude, and certain alternative therapies, as well as the medical means of radiation, chemotherapy, and surgery. I also sensed Him telling me that I was not going to be a cancer survivor, but a cancer overcomer. After using all these means, after surgery the doctors miraculously found the cancer not merely reduced, but completely gone! God has added to my own life message a testimony of God's healing and overcoming power over distress and disease that has been an encouragement to many.

## GOD ENCOURAGES US SO THAT WE MIGHT ENCOURAGE OTHERS

*"Blessed be the God and Father of our Lord Jesus Christ, the Father of mercies and God of all comfort; who comforts us in all our affliction so that we may be able to comfort those who are in any affliction with the comfort with which we ourselves are comforted by God"*
(2 Corinthians 1:3-4, NASB).

God comforts us so that we might comfort others. The growth we experience from our own afflictions is not just for our benefit, but for others as well. We develop compassion for those who are hurting. We suffer with them and really know how they feel because we have been there ourselves. Whatever pain you have experienced, you can identify with others in pain because, to paraphrase an old folk song, you have "walked a mile in their shoes." As Ezekiel shared the bitterness of the Jews in Babylonian exile, he could say, "I sat where they sat" (Ezekiel 3:15, KJV).

If you have been treated unjustly and have overcome and forgiven those who hurt you, rather than becoming bitter, you can minister with compassion to those who are victims of injustice and be motivated by holy anger to stir change and administration of justice. If you have been through a divorce, but have been healed of your deep hurts and have been able to forgive your former spouse, you have a message to share with others who suffer through the pain of divorce. If you have had an abortion and have agonized with guilt over your decision, but have found the love and forgiveness of God, you have a message to share with others who have had abortions or who are considering abortions. If you have lost a spouse or child or parent or close friend, you can sympathize with others who have lost loved ones. Whatever you have been through—abuse, divorce, death, failure, financial ruin, disability, deep sin, addiction—God can turn it around for good, not just for yourself, but for others.

Robert, one of my seminary students, as a teenager had been arrested several times and was heavily involved in substance abuse. He became a Christian and was set free from drugs and alcohol. He later became a probation officer in the city of Chicago and an associate pastor of a church. His testimony became: "Once a juvenile delinquent himself, Robert is now working with delinquents as a juvenile probation officer. Once arrested for breaking into a court house, Robert is now employed at a court house."[42] Since that time he has advanced to become a prison chaplain.

Now this does not mean that you have to go to prison to help those in prison. It does not mean that you have to have an abortion in order to help others with abortions, or that you have to have been an alcoholic or homosexual in order to help alcoholics or homosexuals. But it does mean that God often weaves His purposes into the fabric of the failures and trials of our lives. By His grace we can re-channel our focus away from our painful experience toward what He wants to accomplish through our lives.

## GOD BLESSES US TO BLESS OTHERS

What if you have no spectacular conversion? Do you have to go out and sin so that you can have a great testimony and be used by God? Not at all. You can share how God prepared and nurtured you and led you in His path to faith. God told Abraham, "I will bless you, and make your name great, and so you shall be a blessing" (Gen. 12:2, NASB). If you have been blessed by God, you can bless others.

For example, if you have been successful financially, you can provide for the needs of others, show people in financial difficulty how they can become financially free, and demonstrate principles of financial success. My wife and I committed ourselves early in our marriage to get out of debt and stay out of debt. For more than 30 years of our marriage we have been able to stay debt-free. We may not have always possessed the newest and greatest and fanciest, but God has always taken care of us. Even though we are by no means wealthy, we have been able to share with many others how they can become financially free. If you are financially free, God can use you to help others to financial freedom.

In a similar way, if you grew up in a stable Christian home, you can share that stability with others. If you have a strong, loving marriage, your marriage can be a role model for others. In whatever way your life has been enriched by God, you can bear witness of what God has accomplished. We are not blessed by God merely for our own sake, but to bless others.

God's purposes for your life are revealed both in your blessings and in your experiences of overcoming deep trials. These form your life message for others. The old hymn appropriately expresses the prayer of our heart, "Make me a blessing to someone today."

## Identify Your Life Scripture

My life Scripture ever since I was in high school has been Philippians 3:10-14:

> I want to know Christ and the power of his resurrection and the fellowship of sharing in his sufferings, becoming like him in his death, and so, somehow, to attain to the resurrection from the dead. Not that I have already obtained all this, or have already been made perfect, but I press on to take hold of that for which Christ Jesus took hold of me. Brothers, I do not consider myself yet to have taken hold of it. But one thing I do: Forgetting what is behind and straining toward what is ahead, I press on toward the goal to win the prize for which God has called me heavenward in Christ Jesus.

Since these verses are written by the Apostle Paul and my name is Paul, this Scripture has been especially meaningful to me. This Scripture defines who I am, who God has called me to be, and the life mission to which He has called me more than any another. I have a passion for knowing Jesus Christ more and more.

When Paul wrote these words, he had been a Christian more than 20 years. Yet he prayed, ". . . that I may know Him." Didn't Paul know Jesus? Hadn't he had a personal encounter with Jesus on the Damascus road beyond anything most of us have experienced? Hadn't he seen a vision of Jesus and heard His voice? And yet he pines, "I want to know Him more."

"I want to know more of the power of His resurrection." Had he not experienced the power of the resurrection? Had he not healed the sick, cast out demons, been caught up into the third heaven, spoken in tongues more than anyone else, even raised the dead? And yet he prays for more resurrection power.

He prays, "that I may know the fellowship of His sufferings." Had he not been beaten, slandered, persecuted, gone without food and water, shipwrecked, and much more? Yet he prays to share more of the sufferings of Jesus.

This is my heart—to know Jesus Christ more and more, to press on for all that God has for me, and to lead others to this higher and deeper and fuller life in Christ. This is the passion that consumes me and drives me.

My second life Scripture is Ephesians 4:11-13, which I have cited earlier. Issuing out of my passion to help others know the depth of fullness of life in Christ, is my sense of calling to equip believers to do the work of ministry. Combining these verses with Philippians 3:10-14, my life mission statement is "to equip believers for ministry to build up the body of Christ by leading others to a higher, deeper, and fuller life in Christ."

What is your life Scripture, the passage of Scripture that defines God's meaning or purpose for your life, the verses that are the most meaningful to you in the Bible? Have you discovered what your life mission is, and have you written it out?

Think about what key Scriptures have had major impact upon your life and your motivation for living. Write down those Scriptures. Identify the message that God would have you to share with others based on those verses. Write out a mission statement based on that message God has placed in your heart. Put that on a card before you where you can see it—by your desk, on your refrigerator, on a mirror in your bedroom or bathroom, on the dashboard of your car.

## WRITE DOWN YOUR EXPERIENCES AND LIFE MESSAGE

In the last chapter we mentioned the importance of writing down your vision and making it plain on tablets. Writing out your life message makes it clearer to you and enables you to communicate it better with others. As Francis Bacon once asserted, "Writing makes an exact man." Keep a journal of your experiences and insights that God has taught you. You never know when God might use those insights to help others.

One of my doctoral students, Sandra Clifton, at one time before her conversion had been a New Age psychic with her own TV show. She committed her life to Christ and was set free from her bondage to occult powers. Some people think psychic powers are a gift from God. From her own experience, she knows otherwise. She experienced fear, depression, oppression, deception, and enslavement, not a blessing from God. As a result, she has written a book about her experiences and liberation from the occult entitled *From New Age to New Life*, and now she is teaching seminars and planting a church along with her husband.[43]

Gene McMath, a classmate of mine from many years ago, accidentally drove his truck over a 300 foot cliff in Colorado. He was rescued and miraculously recovered from a near-death experience. Since then, he has been sharing his life message about his recovery and spiritual journey through music, public speaking and, most recently, a book entitled *Twice Rescued: A New View of Life from the Bottom of the Cliff.*[44]

If you have writing skills, you can write an article or book about your life message to share with others. If you don't have writing skills, you can write down your ideas in a journal or compile your thoughts and have someone else with a writing background or English major formulate and edit it for you. Or you can read books on how to write or go to a writing workshop or seminar to learn the skills. If it won't interest a major publisher, you can self-publish for just a few hundred dollars. Of course, not everyone should write a book about their experiences. As A.W. Tozer once quipped, "You should only write a book if you have to." You need to have the skills and the passion or burden to do so.

## FROM WHERE HAS GOD BROUGHT YOU?

My life message has developed over many years through the experiences of life. Throughout this entire book I am sharing illustrations of the life message God has given to me. I suffered deep chronic depression, but God enabled me to overcome. He replaced my poor self-image with His image. He took a seeming failure in ministry and has used me for His kingdom and glory. I suffered heavy financial reverses, but have been amply provided for by God. I was a college dropout, but now by God's enabling I have two earned doctoral degrees. He took me in the middle of a mid-life crisis and turned my life around for His sake. God has turned around my weaknesses, failures, shortcomings, mistakes, and made something good out of them.

As someone has said, "God takes our *miss*steps and makes them *His* steps." What has God done in you? From where has He brought you? What is God doing in and through your life now? Let God show you His life message in you. You can find your niche in the unique things God has accomplished in and through your life.

Your life message will open doors of service to others for the sake of the kingdom of God.

## FOR FURTHER REFLECTION

1. What failures have you had? How did you overcome?

2. What wounds, sorrows, or losses have you suffered? How were you healed?

3. What struggles, temptations, or difficulties have you had? How did you gain the victory?

4. What blessing have you received from the Lord? How can you share them with others?

5. Whom do you know who has gone through similar experiences? How can you minister to them?

6. What are your life Scriptures? How do they define and motivate your life message?

7. Write out your personal life mission statement—what God has called you to do.

# Discover Your Abilities, Interests, Gifts, and Personality

If God gives you a dream, vision or burden, He will supply the necessary abilities and resources to accomplish it. Those abilities may come through your talents, skills, gifts and personality. Aristotle once said, "Where your talents and the needs of the world cross, there lies your vocation."[45]

## Your Talents, Skills, and Experiences

Your natural talents are abilities, tendencies or aptitudes for which you seem to be naturally inclined. The ability may come easily for you, or it may appear to be inherited. These are God-given, but may not always be recognized because they were present or latent in some form before you made a commitment to Christ. They are a part of God's purposes for your life. God is the Divine Chess master, engineering your abilities and experiences throughout your life to accomplish His purposes.

Paul was endowed with Roman citizenship from birth. That privilege could be taken for granted. But many years later it opened up doors for Paul to be a channel of God's use and got him out of tight places.

Your experiences of life, as mentioned earlier, shape your life message. Even long before my call to ministry at the age of twelve, God was using seemingly random experiences of to prepare the way. When I was about ten years old, the church I grew up in built a new facility and was getting rid of old furnishings. My father, who always had a penchant to collect things for possible future use, took the old pulpit to use for storage. I recall that I would stand on a box behind the pulpit and pretend to preach. Even at that young age, God, in His divine foreknowledge, was stirring me to preach. Further, my experiences of memorizing Scripture in elementary school Vacation Bible School and participating on Bible quiz teams as a high school student prepared me and molded me for a calling as a teacher.

Your skills have also been divinely engineered. God provided you opportunities to learn and develop certain skills, gain knowledge and experience in specific areas, of which you had no idea and saw no connection with what you perceived God was doing in your life. In Exodus 35:30-35, God ordained and arranged Bezalel to be filled with the Spirit for all craftsmanship—Spirit-endowed artistic abilities.

One of those skills I had acquired while I was a teenager was organization, but I did not realize it. In fact, when I started in ministry I hated administration, "adminis-trivia," as I called it. If you would have told me then that several years later I would be a Christian school administrator and eventually a university administrator, I would have told you that you were crazy. Yet when I look back on my teenage years, I can see that God was developing in me organizational skills. I liked to work with charts, especially as a basketball manager keeping statistics for our high school games. And although I have never been fastidious, I liked to keep things organized at home. Having grown up in the depression, my parents were packrats, saving stacks of all sorts of things. I too am a packrat, but the difference between me and my parents is that I am an organized packrat. My parents put things in piles; I put them in piles and files.

My organizational abilities were recognized by a public school superintendent who was a member of a church where I served as pastor. He asked me to serve on a School Accountability Committee as an adjunct to the school board and then on the Five-Year Planning Committee. Little did I know that God was preparing me for becoming a Christian School administrator and a university administrator. Further, this church had a tradition of the pastor giving a children's sermon each Sunday. I hated children's sermons and agonized over preparing them. But people grew to enjoy my children's sermons more than my regular sermons! Again, little did I know that God was preparing me to be able to communicate well with children as a Christian school administrator.

## *The Death of Our Abilities*

The problem with our natural talents and acquired skills is that because of the Fall and the natural sinfulness of humankind, they are often tainted with and influenced by our fleshly nature. There is too much of self, of ego, of flesh, to be used effectively by God. These abilities may be given by God, but because we are too prone to believing WE have attained them, they must be transformed by God. As Watchman Nee writes in his classic book *The Normal Christian Life*, our natural abilities must be cruci-fied, resurrected, transformed and sanctified.[46] Likewise, Alan Redpath has said, "Most of us, God forgive us, are too big for God to use. We are too full of our own schemes and of our own way of doing things. God has to humble us and break us and empty us."[47] What we think are our strengths may end up being our weaknesses. Our talents and skills can be a liability to God unless we submit them to His hand of surgery and remolding. Sometimes our usefulness *for* God can jeopardize our use-fulness *by* God. Paul was trained as a rabbi, but he had to go through wilderness experiences, and be retrained before he could be fully used by God as an apostle. Like Moses' rod, God can use our talents if we are willing to throw them down, and let Him take over and transform them.

I had opportunity to be involved in public speaking and performance many times while growing up. As early as the fifth grade, I was given the lead part in the school musical—I was the sandman! I also sang as a child in my church and was a song leader (except for an interlude while my voice was changing!). I was part of a teen folk gospel group in the 1960s. My church gave me the opportunity to preach my first sermon when I was 17. As a senior in high school as an officer in the National Honor Society I was asked to speak at an all school convocation with about 1000 students, parents and teachers present. And I received an ovation after speaking my first sentence! I became active in youth ministry at the age of 19. So I became quite skilled and at ease with public speaking and presentations in front of a large group of people.

However, on one speaking occasion when I was about 21, I started getting butterflies and jitters. My knees started knocking and I became tongue-tied, babbling incoherently (and I wasn't speaking in tongues!). This had never happened to me before. As I prayed about it, the Lord showed me that Paul King had to die; I had to be crucified; MY ability had to go—so that it became not Paul King speaking for Jesus, but Jesus speaking through Paul King. I could no longer be proud of my speaking ability, for it was what He had done in me. Then God could restore my speaking ability and use me more effectively for His kingdom. I have gone through stages like this in other aspects of my life as well.

On the other hand, we must be careful not to let our abilities limit what God wants to do through our lives. Oswald Chambers cautions,

"One of the greatest hindrances in coming to Jesus is the excuse of temperament. We make our temperament and natural affinities barriers to coming to Jesus."[48] In fact, God loves to take our weaknesses and make them strengths. Then it is His doing and not our own. If we let God have His way with us, Chambers says, "He will make a holy experiment out of me, and God's experiments always succeed."[49]

## Your Interests

Oftentimes God uses your interests and your hobbies to provide keys for finding your niche. What do you enjoy doing with your time? Through the years, I have had two main hobbies—writing and genealogy. I have loved to write ever since I was in junior high school. I kept journals and wrote down snatches of ideas. Although it was many years before my writing skills were honed and my writing career blossomed, my interest in writing set the stage for eventually opening doors to write for publication.

Related to this was my absorption with researching family history. I had always been interested in genealogy, but when my brother-in-law Jim, who had been a family history buff, passed away, it seemed to me to be appropriate to continue his effort to research my wife's family history. I dove in head first, attending genealogy seminars, making several trips to the National Archives and Daughters of American Revolution Library, pouring over family letters, journals, and documents, visiting courthouses and graveyards. It is like detective work, each new piece of information providing new hints or dead ends, or fresh direction. It can be addictive and fascinating! I found out my wife's ancestral connections with Daniel Boone, native American Indians, Swiss barons, Revolutionary and Civil Wars, the Irish potato famine, and even Robert the Bruce, King of Scots. (Even though my surname is King, she is the one with greater royalty!)

I don't have much time these days to research family history, but my fondness for research paved the way for me to work on a doctoral dissertation that included similar biographical and historical research, as well as research for my first four books. My love for research and discovering new information, history and facts has resulted in more than 50 publications. A friend and colleague has called me "a research machine." God used my hobbies to further my career and open new doors for my niche.

## Your Spiritual Gifts

Our spiritual gifts are abilities endowed by the Holy Spirit, not on the basis of education, merit, or spirituality, but by God's grace. According to Romans 12:3-6, those gifts are given according to measures of grace or faith. The gifts may be latent or in embryonic form and may need to be developed. Gifts need to be stirred up. Paul counsels Timothy, ""Fan into flame the gift of God, which is in you through the laying on of my hands" (2 Timothy 1:6; see also 1 Timothy 4:14).

The spiritual gifts listed in Romans 12:6-8 are often referred to as motivational gifts, gifts that provide an inner motivation for interest, action and fulfillment:

> Since we have gifts that differ according to the grace given to us, each of us is to exercise them accordingly: if prophecy, according to the proportion of his faith; if service, in his serving; or he who teaches, in his teaching; or he who exhorts, in his exhortation; he who gives, with liberality; he who leads, with diligence; he who shows mercy, with cheerfulness (NASB).

## Characteristics of Motivational Gifting

For a comprehensive listing, study and test for motivational gifts, I highly recommend the Don and Katie Fortune's book, *Discover Your God-Given Gifts*. See the Appendix for additional resources for discovering your spiritual gifts. These are some of the general characteristics of each of the seven motivational gifts. Different teachers may describe them in a variety of ways, but this is a summary of the categories.[50]

### Prophecy/Perceiver

- Likes to talk and is often outspoken
- Tends to like literature, poetry, art, drama, and or music – things which express feelings, a flair for the dramatic
- Points out things that are wrong & wants to make them right
- Sees everything in black or white, no gray areas
- Tends to be impulsive i.e., emotional— speak out without thinking,
- Sometimes jumps to conclusions
- Tends to dwell on the negative rather than the positive things, moody
- Has perceptiveness
- Is intuitive

## *Teaching*

- Enjoys books and reading, studying, doing research and thinking
- Likes logic, analysis, systematizing
- Likes to check things out and see if they are really true
- Accurate—pays attention to details
- Likes things in order
- Tends to be less practical
- Can become dogmatic

## *Serving*

- Likes to help people do things
- Tends to be practical
- Likes hands-on work
- Likes to be active, to "do" a lot of things
- Likes to be with other people and doing things with them
- Has much physical endurance and energy to do everything
- Tends to be a supporter
- May become too busy helping others, neglect one's own responsibilities or family

## *Exhorting*

- Likes to encourage, excite, persuade people
- Positive thinker, optimistic
- Likes to give practical advice, tell a person how to solve a problem ("here's what you should do. . .").
- Likes to talk with people one-on-one, face-to-face.
- Motivates people with words and is often a good communicator.
- Can be opinionated and overly self-confident.

## *Giving*

- May be good with math and/or money and finances
- Often good with business—good at making money.
- Likes to give or lend people money or things.
- Thinks in terms of "What will it cost?"

- Enterprising abilities like lemonade stand, neighborhood shows, candy or cake sales, paper route, lawn mowing.
- May be overly generous.
- Can tend to manipulate or control.

### Leading/Administration

- Likes to take charge, to get people to do things.
- Likes to organize, plan.
- Task-oriented— likes to get things done & see things accomplished.
- Schedules and plans are important.
- A place for everything.
- Organizes peers into teams for play, work, or group projects.
- Keeps "Post-It" notes in business by continually writing notes
- Often not people-oriented enough

### Mercy/Compassion

- Feels for those who are hurting and suffering.
- Likes to help them feel better.
- Tends to go on emotions and feelings
- Likes being with people one-on-one rather than in big groups
- Has inclination to take up for the underdog
- May be over-trusting or overly-sympathetic

Which of these are most characteristic of you? One or two of these motivational giftings will probably stand out to you. It is these areas of gifting that most interest you and from which you find the greatest fulfillment.

This indicates further that your motivational gifts may lead you to a particular vocation in which you find the greatest significance and fulfillment. The chart on the following page lists a few of the common types of vocation identified with each motivational gift.

## Prophecy/Perceiver

- Evangelist
- Prophetic preacher
- Artist
- Musician
- Political or social activist
- Media/communication
- Public speaking
- Poet
- Lawyer
- Actor

## Teaching

- Teaching
- Librarian
- Research
- Communication
- Scientist
- Analyst

## Exhorting

- Sales
- Evangelism
- Counseling
- Politics
- Public speaking
- Musician
- Coaching
- Advertising
- Cheerleading

## Serving

- Food service
- Mechanics
- Construction
- Public services
- Laborer
- Technician
- Clerical
- Book keeper

## Giving

- Businessman
- Charity organizations
- Fundraiser
- Insurance
- Real Estate
- Accounting
- Book keeping
- Enterprises

## Administration, Leading

- Business
- Management
- Administration
- Foreman
- Politics

## Mercy (Compassion)

- Social services
- Medical profession
- Counseling
- Ministers
- Social worker
- Care for elderly, young, prisoners, handicap, underprivileged, abused

After considering the characteristics and related vocations of each motivational gift, you can discover your own areas of gifting. What gift do you think is most needed in the church? That may be the prime gifting God has given you.

Just remember that your area of gifting is not a guarantee of your fulfillment or success. Don and Katie Fortune observe that

> many other factors besides giftedness contribute to success in any field: talents, special abilities, training, education, background, emotional stability, dependability, commitment, adaptability, and so forth. A person with little gifting in an area can succeed because of his eagerness to learn and apply himself, whereas a person with great gifting in the same area can fail because of poor attitude, laziness, indifference, or unwillingness to make a nine-to-five commitment. . . . Individual circumstances, opportunities, and anointing will also help determine your actual choice.[51]

## YOUR PERSONALITY

God also uses your personality to accomplish His purposes for your life! Your personality traits are part of who God has made you to be. Like our skills and talents, God may need to adjust our personality traits to become, as Tim LaHaye writes, "Spirit-controlled temperaments." LaHaye comments, "This temperament modification is to be expected. . . . The degree of modification in a person's temperament will be in direct proportion to the filling of his life with the Spirit."[52]

Many different surveys by both secular and Christian sources use the four basic personality traits to give an index of who you are. Others are critical of stereotyping people by these temperaments or making them into a form of fortune-telling. My counsel is that they can be used to help you understand yourself and others as long as you do not stereotype or box yourself in with such typing. They can be helpful in finding out what kinds of work or vocations for which you are well-suited. Some have seen in these four personality traits the four faces of Christ in the four Gospels and the four-faced creatures in the books of Ezekiel 1 and Revelation 4.

| Personality Colors | Red Personality | Yellow Personality | Blue Personality | Green Personality |
|---|---|---|---|---|
| Gary Smalley Animal Types | Lion Captain | Otter Social Director | Beaver Navigator | Golden Retriever Steward |
| L.E.A.D. Personality Inventory[53] | Leader | Expressor | Analyst | Dependable |
| Tim LaHaye Temperaments | Choleric | Sanguine | Melancholy | Phlegmatic |
| DISC Profile | D | I | C | S |
| DISC characteristics | Direct Dominant Demanding Decisive Daring Driver | "I, me" Influencing Impulsive Interest in people Inspiration Intuitive Ideas | Competent Cautious Compliant Conscientious Critical thinking Chart Maker Creator | Steady Stable Security Status Quo Supporter Sincerity Sympathy |
| Ministry Type | Prophet's heart | Evangelist's heart | Teacher's heart | Pastor's heart |
| Four Faces in Ezekiel | Lion | Eagle | Man | Ox |
| Gospel Profile of Jesus | Matthew Jesus as King | John Jesus as Son of God | Luke Jesus as Man | Mark Jesus as Servant |
| Biblical Example | Paul | Peter | Luke | Abraham[54] |

These are just a few of the personality models and styles that can help you to understand your personality, behavior, and interests. Among others are the Myers-Briggs Temperament Types, Bolton's Social Styles, and many more.[55]

The Red/Leader/Choleric/D personalities tend to be bold, aggressive, and decisive, and can make effective leaders if they are not too overbearing or authoritarian. Yellow/Expressor/Sanguine/I personalities are party animals, out-going and effective in people-oriented types of work, so long as they as are not manipulating or too impulsive. The Blue/Analytical/Melancholy/C personalities are strong at task-oriented types of work and maintaining order and organization if they are not too picky or introspective. The Green/Dependable/Phlegmatic/S personalities are hospitable, caring persons who try to get along with everybody, but can let people take advantage of them. They do well with routines.

In Gary Smalley's Personality scheme, the lion is the bold ruler, the captain who takes charge. The otter is the playful, fun-loving social director. The beaver is the industrious, competent navigator to bring quality and control to life, and the golden retriever is the warm, laid-back, loyal friend and steward of life.[56]

Of course, we are a blend of all four personality characteristics, but usually one or two of these areas stand out. All of our temperaments, as Tim LaHaye points out, need to be guided and transformed by the Holy Spirit.[57]

These traits also give an indication of what kind of work would not be fulfilling. For example, a person with the Ruler type of personality is not going to be comfortable with a repetitive or routine situation. An Expressor personality will not be happy or effective in detail task-oriented type of work. An Analytical task-oriented person may not be comfortable in a social or highly people-orientation situation. Those with the Dependable trait do not usually like to be in charge or have a lot of changes in their lives.

If you are miserable in your present job, it could be that you are not in a job that suits your personality or abilities. You can remain faithful in that job, but be praying for God's guidance and searching for new opportunities more suited to your personality and abilities.

## Beyond Your Gifts and Personality

One caution: do not limit finding your niche to what you are now and the gifts you have discovered that you have. God wants to take us beyond where we are. He wants to stretch us and remold us, and always take us a little farther out into the deep. He takes us beyond our comfort zones. So just because you don't think you have a gifting in a certain area don't conclude that you cannot find God's purposes in it. God may want to impart a new gift to you. He may want to do something entirely new.

Further, don't think that your personality limits you. God wants to change and round out your personality. He may want you to develop in other personality traits to balance you out. Jesus was the perfect blend of all personalities, knowing when to be laid back and when to be a forceful leader, knowing when to withdraw and when to be expressive. So God wants to move you beyond yourself.

My wife Kathy does not usually consider herself the leader type of personality, but she has a servant's heart. She would rather teach a Sunday School class than to be a Sunday School Superintendent or a Christian education director. She would rather sing in a choir than lead a choir. However, as a pastor's wife, she was stretched and had to wear many hats and do all of the above and more! She actually became versatile and gained some valuable leadership and administrative qualities. Later, with a degree in elementary education she took a job working in a Christian book, educational and office supply store. It was not long before she was promoted to a position as Education Department Head in the largest store in the company, leading the department and directing others. It has stretched her, but she has done well. She actually found that years after taking one of these spiritual gifts surveys, administration/leadership actually became one of her gifts, when on the same survey a decade earlier this was not one of her strengths.

Don't let the results of a gifts survey or a personality test box you in or keep you from becoming all that God wants to develop in you and through you. Let God stretch you and remold you in His image, whatever shape that may end up becoming.

## FOR FURTHER REFLECTION

1. What are your talents? Have you surrendered them to God?

2. What are your skills? Can you identify how God has used or could use them for His purposes?

3. What are your spiritual gifts? How can God use them to fulfill His purposes?

4. Which personality traits are most like you? In what ways have they been transformed into God's image? How can God use your particular personality?

# Receive Confirmation from God and Others

As a teenager, I received a call to ministry from the Lord at an evangelist's tent meeting. I thought that call was to be an evangelist, and so eventually I joined the staff of Young Life and experienced a successful youth evangelistic ministry. Yet I noticed that so many of the teenagers I led to Christ seemed to fall back in their faith. I recognized the need of follow up and discipleship. Thus I changed the focus of my ministry to teens to more teaching and discipling. Some of the other staff leaders commented to me at a retreat, "Paul, you are not an evangelist." I felt deflated! "What do you mean, I am not an evangelist? I have been called by God." They responded, "Don't you see, Paul? You are a teacher!" It never dawned on me until others recognized it in me and revealed it to me. It changed my whole focus of ministry from then on. I wanted to help people understand what the Word of God means and how we can apply it to our lives in order to become strong in faith.

When we receive recognition and confirmation of our calling, we can step out in faith and act in confidence. It is valuable for your calling to be recognized and affirmed by others, receiving their blessing, and the permission and release of those in authority over you. The Scripture frequently speaks of letting everything be established by the witness of two or three (2 Corinthians 13:1; see also Matthew 18:18-20).

## MEANS OF CONFIRMATION

This recognition may come through various means: by supernatural communications from God such as impressions, visions, dreams, prophecy, word of knowledge or wisdom, through more natural means of seeking the counsel of mature Christians, or through the process of discipleship, mentoring, and spiritual direction.

### Supernatural Communication

It was while the prophets and teachers, the leadership team, of the church of Antioch were praying that the Holy Spirit revealed to the body of leaders God's call to Paul and Barnabas to launch out into apostolic ministry (Acts 13:2-3). Paul wrote to Timothy: "Timothy, my son, I give you this instruction in keeping with the prophecies once made about you, so that by following them you may fight the good fight. . . . Do not neglect your gift, which was given you through a prophetic message when the body of elders laid their hands on you" (1 Timothy 1:18; 4:14). Some months later he wrote Timothy again, exhorting, "For this reason I remind you to fan into flame the gift of God, which is in you through the laying on of my hands." (2 Timothy 1:6).

Some may think that God does not speak through prophetic words today, but the great 19th century Baptist preacher Charles Spurgeon is an example of someone who received his calling in this way. A preacher by the name of Richard Gill prophesied over him when he was ten years old (even before his conversion), declaring, "This child will one day preach the gospel, and he will preach it before multitudes."[58] A similar incident happened to Oswald Chambers.

You may or may not receive a prophetic word as dramatic as that, but it is possible that God may speak to you in this way. When I was about 20 years old I received prophetic messages from three people on three different occasions, all saying essentially that I would be a "leader of leaders." Since the Scriptures advise, "Every matter must be established by the testimony of two or three witnesses" (2 Cor. 13:1), receiving such a word from three people independently of each other seemed to verify that God was going to do it. Hence, I had the dream of becoming a seminar and conference Bible teacher. For many years the prophecies went unfulfilled, and I began to think that they were false prophecies. It was not until 26 years later that the prophecies began to come true in my life. Then God opened up a door for me to become a professor and seminar teacher, training men and women for ministry. I have had opportunity to teach dozens of seminars on Ministry and Leadership Development and other topics throughout the United States, as well as internationally in Canada, South Africa, Jamaica, the Virgin Islands, Singapore, and Fiji.

God told Daniel his vision was for the distant future (Daniel 8:26; 10:14; 12:9). God may be giving you a vision of the distant future, not

His immediate plans. I know of someone who received a prophetic word that he would go to Columbia to minister. He packed his bags and prepared to go, but it was six years before he actually had the opportunity to go to Columbia. The lesson he learned was never to act on a word without confirmation, no matter how supernatural it may seem. God's timing is not always our timing. Don't be discouraged if your vision does not materialize for many years.

Further, don't force it to happen, or you may end up with an Ishmael. God appeared to Abraham and told him he would have innumerable descendents like the sands of the sea. When his wife could not conceive a child for many years and she was beyond the age of childbearing, they thought they needed to help God out. Ishmael was the outcome—the product of human efforts to accomplish God's purposes, which has resulted in millennia of mid-eastern conflict.

## Counsel and Confirmation from Others

It is important that you receive other confirmation as well, and not go off on your own based only on a prophetic word or impression. If you think you are hearing from God, other mature people in Christ will bear witness. We cannot be Lone Rangers or Rambos going off on our own mission. Richard Foster gives wise counsel in his book *Celebration of Discipline*: "But the knowledge of the direct, active, immediate leading of the Spirit is not sufficient. Individual guidance must yield to corporate guidance."[59] As Proverbs 11:14 advises, "There is safety in a multitude of counselors."

Several years ago, a new position was offered to me. Although the salary package was lower than my current package at the time, the position actually would have been a promotion in other ways, and had great potential for expansion of ministry. I was torn in two directions. The income package was not adequate, yet the opportunity was great. I asked myself and the Lord, "Should I take a step in faith and trust God to provide the lack?"

I have two pastor friends who speak into my life, and I sought them for counsel. They did not make a decision for me, but helped me to consider and evaluate all the factors. They encouraged me to negotiate the salary package. I did so, and with somewhat reluctance was offered some concessions, though still not what we determined we needed. When my wife and I went to meet with them and make the final decision, we had a peace about accepting the position even though it was not the salary package we felt we needed, but we would just trust the Lord to make up the difference. At the last minute, the offer was withdrawn. Though

I was greatly disappointed, and wondered for a time if I had asked for too much, I came to a peace that this job was not what God wanted. Circumstances that emerged nearly two years later confirmed that the position would not have worked out in the long term. Getting counsel from godly, mature men of God who know me and my gifts and calling was vital in the decision-making process.

## *Finding a Mentor, Spiritual Director, or Coach*

This is where having a mentor, spiritual director, or coach is especially invaluable. Each of these is similar and overlaps in function; however, each has a different focus.

- A *mentor* is like a craftsman training an apprentice, equipping you in the skills he or she has, in effect reproducing his or her life in you.
- A *spiritual director* focuses particularly on providing spiritual direction and discernment, leading you closer to God and helping you to hear God.
- A *coach* is more of a facilitator, helping you to accomplish your goals in life.

These roles are not distinct from each other, but thinking about the nuances between them can help you decide which focus you want or need. (See the Appendix for more resources.)

What should you look for in a mentor, spiritual director, or coach? First of all, all three involve a relationship. Look for someone who you can spend some time with, get to know that person, and let that person get to know you. You need someone who knows you inside and out, who is aware of your strengths and weaknesses and can discern your motives. You don't want a "yes-man" (or woman) who will tell you what you want to hear, but rather someone who will tell you what you need to hear, who can genuinely speak the truth in love. You need someone who can give you encouragement, and also rebuke. It needs to be someone you can trust with your life, someone to whom you can be accountable, someone from whom you can take a rebuke or receive direction.

Secondly, look for someone you can look up to, who has maturity, who is not dealing with issues of maturity or character in his or her own life. The wisdom of years and experience of those who have been through the fires of life and emerged sound and strong can be of great insight for decisions in your life. That does not necessarily mean someone older or more educated than you, or someone who is an expert. One of those pastor friends I mentioned earlier is younger than I am and does not even have a degree in Bible or theology. In fact, I was his dormitory wing chaplain in college and performed his wedding! My daughter has babysat his daughters; my son has driven them to school. Yet we have known each other a quarter of a century and he has gained great wisdom and insight both from the business world and from pastoral ministry.

Thirdly, look for someone from whom you can learn—both in instruction and in demonstration. Find someone whom you can observe—watch his or her behavior, actions and reactions, manner of life, as well as way of doing things. Many years ago, I sold jewelry for J.C. Penney. When I started, I didn't know anything about jewelry. I didn't even own any jewelry besides my wedding ring. I went through several hours of training tapes, but what was the most valuable was being on the sales floor, just watching successful sales representatives communicate with customers. I listened and observed and learned from their techniques. Then I began to put them into practice. Eventually, I became one of those top sales people.

One of my students in a course on theological research and writing was especially interested in writing books on inspirational themes. Since I had published several books and articles, he sought me outside of class for spiritual insights and tips on writing and how to become published. We spent time together discussing spiritual matters and strategies for communicating the message on his heart, as well as honing his writing skills. Since that time, he has become an international evangelist and has published several books.

It is often in those mentoring or discipleship relationships that God speaks and gives guidance, rather than by the supernatural means mentioned above. My mentors, guides and coaches have not made my decisions for me, but they have helped me to be aware of the various factors involved in determining the Lord's leading for my life, and have helped to set me in the right direction more precisely.

## When You Don't Receive Confirmation

What about when you think you are being led by the Lord in a certain direction, but you don't get confirmation or approval? What if your spiritual leaders in whom you have confided tell you, "No"? God may be saying through them, "You are headed in the wrong direction." Or He may be saying, "Wait a while." God may want you to become more prepared for His plans for you. Or perhaps He wants you to proceed in a different way. God may have temporary purposes for you that need to be fulfilled before moving on in God's long-term calling.

At the same time, we also recognize that there are rare exceptions to this principle, in which someone has followed guidance they believed from God when others did not. Bruce Olsen, for instance, was turned down by denominational mission agencies, but went to South America on his own and launched a mission that has borne great and lasting fruit.[60] However, the rare exception does not sanction going out on our own without counsel. We will have to hear from the Lord clearly and be walking in close communion with Him in order to trust such leadings.

There may also be times in which mature Christians differ in their counsel. One may say "yes," and another "no." One may counsel in a certain direction; another may lean in a different direction. This is a time of seeking the Lord once again, weighing all the counsel and factors. In the job opportunity I mentioned above, it was actually one of my mentors who was offering me the job. My other pastor friend/mentors were giving cautionary counsel. Now that is a dilemma! Yet as I sought the Lord, He used the counsel of both sides, as well as my wife and circumstances to lead me to the appropriate decision.

## EXERCISE SANCTIFIED JUDGMENT AND SPIRIT-ENLIGHTENED REASONING

*"But if any of you lacks wisdom, let him ask of God, who gives to all men generously and without reproach, and it will be given to him"*
(James 1:5, NASB).

When I first started preaching in my late teens and early 20s, I thought all I needed to do was to pray and then the Holy Spirit would anoint me with the words to speak. Although God sometimes works that way, I found that God is a God of order and planning and does not fly by the seat of His pants. I also discovered that many of my attempts at "being led by the Spirit" were rambling. When I got married, my wife became my best critic of my preaching. I learned that the Holy Spirit is as much in the *preparation* as He is in the *presentation*. God wanted me to learn to engage my mind and understand that the Holy Spirit works through the process of thinking.

The same is true in our decision-making. God wants us to make use of two related aspects of the thinking process: *sanctified judgment* and *Spirit enlightened reasoning*. *Sanctified judgment* means that we have surrendered all to Jesus, and thus we can make a sound judgment free from our own biases and agenda. *Spirit-enlightened reasoning* means that we are seeking clarification from the Holy Spirit as we are thinking through the decision in our minds. Some might think that Spirit and reason are like oil and water, or an oxymoron. However, Paul exhorts the Ephesians, "Be renewed in the spirit of your mind" (Ephesians 4:23). God intends that our mind and spirit work together in tandem. There are three dangers in the use of our minds: 1) trusting our minds too much, 2) trusting our minds too little, 3) having a lazy mind. Although Paul warns us not to think too much of ourselves (Romans 12:3), this does not mean that we should not use our minds. After all, it was God who said, "'Come now, and let us reason together,' says the Lord" (Isaiah 1:18). God wants us to engage our minds, being renewed and led by the Holy Spirit

The great apostle of faith, George Müller, was quite down-to-earth in seeking God's purposes for his life and ministry. He put into practice such sanctified judgment and Spirit-enlightened reasoning. Although he had created several orphan homes along the same street, he was challenged with the need for more space. As was his practice, he planned to spend a week in prayer and the Word about the possibility of moving to another location and starting new building projects. He recorded the advantages and disadvantages and weighed the issues in thought and prayer:

> I was very busy that week and scarcely had time to consider it further. On Monday morning, however, I set apart some hours for prayerful consideration of the subject. I wrote down the reasons which appeared desirable that the Orphan Houses should  be *moved* from Wilson Street, and the reasons *against moving.* . . . After I had spent a few hours in prayer and consideration of the subject, I began to see that the Lord was leading me to build.[61]

He used this practical means of decision-making on several other occasions as well, trusting the Lord to guide his reasoning.

## WEIGHING THE PROS AND CONS

I have practiced Müller's method many times throughout the years as well. It is very helpful to put down in writing the pros and cons. Rather than just mulling them around in my mind, I became more focused and the issues to weigh were made clearer. Sometimes I would meet with a friend or mentor to discuss the advantages and disadvantages.

If you are making a decision that involves your spouse and family, it is important that you get the input of your spouse. Paul counseled, "Submit to one another in the fear of Christ." We need to listen to the counsel and concerns of those affected by our decision. My wife has contributed valuable insights and perspective in the decision-making process, while at the same time supporting the final decision that I believe the Lord has led me to make.

Below is the simple chart I make when considering a decision:

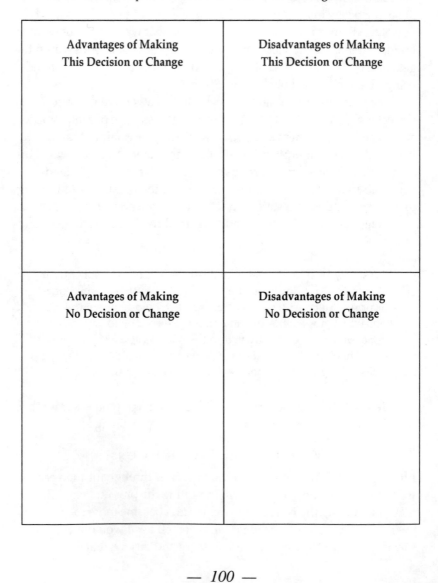

| Advantages of Making<br>This Decision or Change | Disadvantages of Making<br>This Decision or Change |
|---|---|
| **Advantages of Making<br>No Decision or Change** | **Disadvantages of Making<br>No Decision or Change** |

## NARROWING DOWN YOUR OPTIONS

Just a few years ago, my son Chris graduated from college with a major in Theology and Philosophy and a minor in Writing. He desired to spend a year in missions before going on to graduate school. We supported and encouraged his desire, believing that it was from the Lord. But where to go? As he searched out possibilities, nearly a dozen opportunities presented themselves, many of them to unusual and exotic place—the Czech Republic, Afghanistan, Honduras, Venezuela, Thailand, South Korea, Indonesia, Virgin Islands, Guam, and the list goes on. It was overwhelming! How did he narrow down and decide? He thought through the pros and cons of each possibility.

*Financial considerations.* Some of the positions involved raising mission funds. Because our fundraising base was limited, and he also had student educational loans to pay back, these financial issues eliminated positions requiring several thousands of dollars in fundraising. He had taken a college course on Principles of Teaching English as a Second Language (TESL), so he considered several TESL positions, but it would take further time and money to become certified.

*Circumstantial considerations.* Some mission positions required a lot of paperwork and took time to process. As summer approached it was crunch time for making some decisions about fundraising or pursuing an option. Circumstances will often be a sign of open or closed doors. Options that seemed to be bogged down in the process seemed to indicate that God was closing those doors.

*Desire considerations.* Chris wanted to minister overseas in some capacity—preferably teaching Bible or theology in a college, Bible Institute or Christian school.

He was also willing to be a youth worker, or teach other subjects, or serve in another ministerial capacity. There were all kinds of needs—several for TESL, or teaching various subjects. He eliminated those outside his area of interest, even though he could have done them well, and would have been willing to do so if God desired. He had laid all on the altar before the Lord. We encouraged him that his desire was God's desire.

*The Peace of the Lord.* Finally, he narrowed down the options to three—Venezuela, South Korea, and Virgin Islands. Venezuela was still considering him for teaching English, and it would have provided a partial salary, but his heart was in teaching Bible or theology and time was growing short to raise the extra needed funds. Then he was offered the position in the Virgin Islands, teaching G.E.D. classes in Reading and Writing and teaching courses in a new Bible Institute. He was leaning toward accepting the position, but had a few other questions that needed to be answered before saying "yes."

While he was waiting on a response to the questions, the school in South Korea offered him a comparable position teaching Bible and English classes in a Christian school. Both positions provided a modest, but generally adequate stipend without much need for fundraising. Now he was torn in both directions. Panic time! He was on a home missions week with our church when he got the news and had to make a decision within the week. He really didn't know which position to take. My wife and I continued to pray for him for the Lord's guidance, and made ourselves available for counsel, but knew that it had to be his decision. He took some time out one night to go camping and seek the Lord. He came back with a peace that he was to take the position in the Virgin Islands. The finances, circumstances, desire, and peace of the Lord all fell into place.

## CHANGING DIRECTIONS

Sometimes we may have sensed God's leading in one direction, only later to sense His leading in another unrelated direction. We may think that we had missed God's will in the first leading, but, in fact, it was all a part of God's plan. One of my student assistants was a nursing major. She had worked as a nurse's assistant and as a result had an interest in nursing as well as missions. She believed God was leading her to do nursing in conjunction with missions. However, she found prerequisite courses for nursing such as anatomy and physiology too grueling and tedious. But she determined to persevere, in spite of her difficulties. So she canceled a summer mission trip in order focus on her nursing studies, which she found still overwhelming even with concentrated effort.

When the mission team came back from Africa with glowing reports of their experiences, she began to wonder if she had missed God. Her heart yearned even more for missions as a result. Since God had placed this desire in her heart, and she was not finding success or fulfillment in her nursing major, she made an appointment to talk with chair of the theology department. After seeking God she changed her major to psychology with a minor in missions, and sensed the peace of the Lord.

She questioned whether she had misheard the Lord when she believed He wanted her to be a nursing major and wasted her time. I assured her that God often takes us in a circuitous route that seems to be out of the way or does not seem to make sense at the time, but it is all in His plan. I encouraged her that the insights she had learned in her nursing classes thus far would be helpful to her on the mission field. I encouraged her also that God uses the processes and experiences that we go through to give us wisdom for our future. Nothing is wasted in God's economy.

Another college graduate with a degree in international relations spent a year in missions in a very difficult and frustrating circumstance. Then she returned to work on a masters degree in business and worked as a teacher's assistant. After another year of feeling like she was going nowhere, she finally found peace in switching to a masters degree in speech pathology. In both her experiences on the mission field and as a teacher's assistant, she encountered children with speech problems. She found meaning in helping them learn, and it opened up a new door of opportunity to serve in a way she had never thought of before.

## FOR FURTHER REFLECTION

1. What gifts and abilities and callings have your spiritual leaders or others observed in you?

2. Do you have a mentor, spiritual director, coach, pastor, or other mature Christians from whom you receive counsel and spiritual insight?

3. When making an important decision, have you consulted other mature Christians for counsel and confirmation?

4. If you have received a revelation or word from the Lord regarding direction for your life, have you submitted it to Scripture and other mature Christians for evaluation and confirmation?

5. What methodology do you use for making decisions? Do you find it effective?

6. What are the advantages and disadvantages of a decision you need to make? List them on a separate sheet of paper and discuss them with someone.

7. How can you narrow down your options when you have several possible directions or leads?

8. What are the financial issues or circumstances do you need to consider in your decision?

9. What are your desires and interests about this decision as you have submitted them to God and sought His direction? Do you have the peace of the Lord? What do you sense God saying?

# Faithfully Serve Where You Are

*"As you go, preach, saying, "The kingdom of heaven is at hand"*
(Matthew 10:7, KJV).

*"As you are going, therefore, make disciples of all the nations"*
(Matthew 28:19) (my translation).

These Scripture verses indicate to us that as we are going about our routine of life and our daily tasks, we can engage in ministry right where we are. We don't have to go looking for a purpose; we find our purpose as we go about doing what we already know to do. We find our reason for being as we walk in obedience to the insight God has already given us.

## BEGIN TO MINISTER IN YOUR SPHERES OF INFLUENCE

Some people go off somewhere trying to find their calling or build their ministry, rather than ministering and serving right where they are. Now let me be clear that I am not against short-term mission trips. I believe in and support short-term missions. Both of my children have been on short-term mission trips, as well as one of my brothers, and those excursions have had great impact on their lives. It is an eye-opening and life-changing experience, gives people a personal sense of what missions is all about, and leads some into a full-time calling in missions. My brother Glenn, who is in business in computer hardware, software, consultation, and service, has found one of God's purposes through his life using his skills on several short-term mission trips.

However, for some people, going on a short-term mission is a way of showing that they have done something great or worthwhile, because they have not found fulfillment where they are. It is important to note that Jesus said, "You shall be My witnesses both in Jerusalem, and in all Judea and Samaria, and even to the remotest parts of the earth" (Acts 1:8, NASB). We need to begin our witness for Christ, our ministry, our calling right in our own Jerusalem, and let God take us in His way and timing to the uttermost parts of the earth. Begin in your own Jerusalem and then let God spread your ministry outward.

## *The Core of Our Sphere of Influence*

Our sphere of influence is made up of the people around us whose lives we influence—the relationships in our lives. It begins with those who are closest to you—your family and closest friends. Some people go long distances to find a ministry, but your ministry begins with those closest to you. I know of people who will reach out to help others outside of their family, but fail to minister to the needs right at home. I know a man who often goes out and fixes broken down appliances and cars for others, but neglects his own house and lets it get run down. The greatest opportunity for discipleship is right in your home. If you are married and/or have children, your first calling and ministry is to your spouse and children.

When Nehemiah led the rebuilding of the walls of Jerusalem, he instructed each family to repair the section of wall near to them (Nehemiah 3). When threat of attack loomed, he stationed people by families to protect the wall where they were, and instructed them, "Fight for your brothers, your sons, your daughters, your wives and your houses" (Nehemiah 4:14, NASB). If we each will build and protect the portion that is near to us, the walls of our lives will be rebuilt and strengthened, and our families will remain intact.

Since I am the oldest of five children, many years ago I did a study of "firstborn" in Scripture. One thing I discovered is that the firstborn ordinarily gets a double portion of the inheritance! (But I haven't told my father yet, so that he can change his will accordingly). Seriously, the real intent of the double portion is that the firstborn son usually had responsibility for caring for the rest of the family if the father died. Therefore, he needed a double portion to provide for the needs of the extended family, as well as his own wife and children. God revealed me that he was calling me as the firstborn of my family to take spiritual responsibility for my brothers and sister, parents and in-laws, and their families. I asked the Lord, "How I accomplish that when they are spread all over the United States?" He showed me that I could do so by regularly interceding for them daily, making myself available, and encouraging them when I can.

Maybe you are not the physical firstborn in your family, but you are firstborn spiritually—you are a believer in Jesus Christ. You can minister to them in many ways—intercede regularly for them, be available, find ways to show a servant's heart to them, encourage them through cards, phone, e-mail, etc. Don't preach at them; just offer your friendship, and provide counsel when asked.

## The Sphere of the Church

The next sphere of influence is to the Church—especially the local Body of Christ where God has placed you. Paul tells us, "Now you are the body of Christ, and each one of you is a part of it" (1 Corinthians 12:27). As mentioned in an earlier chapter, God's purposes for our lives will be fulfilled as a part of the Church, the Body of Christ. What is your function in the Body of Christ? What needs can you fill in your local church or the Church-at-large? Do not feel as though you have nothing to offer. Do not be concerned that others will not recognize your abilities. Some of the most important functions are those that are not seen or considered noble. Every ability and skill can be used for the sake of the kingdom of God.

## The Sphere of Social and Work Relationships

The next sphere of influence is to your co-workers—those with whom you work or go to school or have frequent contact—perhaps those in your bowling league or families in your son's baseball club or daughter's soccer league. There are a multitude of contacts we have with people who have great needs all around us. Jesus said, "The fields are white unto harvest." This means that the harvest is ready for reaping. Again, He proclaimed, "The harvest is great but the workers are few." The needs are there; we just need to recognize them and perceive the call of God.

One of my students had a goal of becoming a Navy CIS lawyer. When I talked with her about her ministry, she replied that signing and dancing in worship at her church were her ministries. I agreed that they were a part of her ministry, but that God also had a ministry for her as a lawyer. Like so many people, she was divorcing her secular life from her church life. I shared with her that God wanted to use her for His kingdom in her secular job as well.

As I mentioned earlier, several years ago I served a bi-vocational pastor, working for J.C. Penney full-time selling jewelry while pastoring a small congregation. I had many opportunities to share my faith and minister to fellow employees and customers alike. I actually would have counseling sessions during my breaks and lunch hours. I ministered to people whose lives I never would have touched as a full-time pastor.

And the Lord blessed my sales, making me one of the top sales people. In commission sales, there is a lot of in-fighting over who gets the commission for the sale. Because of my success, sometimes I was accused of taking someone else's sale. For the sake of peace and Christ's reputation, there were times that I gave credit for the sale to another person, even though I knew that I deserved it. A hundred dollars in commission for a sale was not worth causing bitterness or casting doubt on my integrity. And the Lord blessed me even more for doing it.

### *The Sphere of Divine Encounters*

Then there are the "divine encounters," the seemingly random contacts that you have with people that provide an opportunity to share the gospel and the love of Jesus Christ with others. When I travel by air, I usually am busy reading, studying, grading, or writing on my laptop. But there have been occasions I have had opportunity to share my faith with someone sitting next to me on the plane. Once I had opportunity to lead a French teacher to Christ. On another occasion when I was in college, a Jewish woman observed me studying Hebrew, and was amazed that a young Gentile would want to study her sacred language. We had a fascinating conversation about the Bible and about Jesus. As I was traveling to teach a seminar on Ministry and Leadership Development at a church and Bible Institute, a woman who was a business leadership training coach became interested in what I do, because it was similar to what she did in the business world. On yet another occasion I had opportunity to pray with a woman who had a fear of flying.

Wherever we go, if we are available to the Lord and alert to the Holy Spirit's promptings, we can be used by God to touch the lives of others. Watch for open doors.

As you are faithful to using the abilities God has given you and fulfilling the tasks He has given you, God will lead you into new dimensions. I once heard Desmond Evans, who as a little boy experienced the move of God in the Welsh revival, speak about the ways of God. With his deep Welsh accent he affirmed, "God can and does take His people to unusual places for the excellence of His name."

I have found that so true through the years. I never in my life sought or expected to teach or preach in places like Harlem, Jamaica, Singapore, or among Zulus in South Africa, or to train more than a hundred pastors in the Fiji Islands. Yet as I continued to do what God had given me to do, He has opened the doors and brought about the opportunities. If you will serve the relationships in your life, God will open doors for you as well.

## WHEN YOU FEEL RESTLESS

Earlier I mentioned that restlessness may be a sign of a burden God has given you. However, I would also caution, don't move too soon. Restlessness may not always be God's doing. Sometimes it is our human flesh, wanting something more, acting on impulse. If you are the kind of person who acts on impulse, it is especially important that you take care not to step out ahead of God.

The best course of action is to plan to stay for the long haul, but be ready to pick up and go at a moment's notice when you hear from God. Dietrich Bonhoeffer commented, "It is the mark of a grown-up man, as compared with a callow youth, that he finds his center of gravity wherever he happens to be at the moment, and however much he longs for the object of his desire, it cannot prevent him from staying at his post and doing his duty."[62]

## WHEN YOU FEEL USELESS

Oswald Chambers has been especially helpful to me in understanding God's purposes for me in the dry times, the times I don't see God at work in and through my life, the times that I feel like God has benched me. He says, "Never allow the thought, 'I am of no use where I am,' because you certainly can be of no use where you are not."[63] He warns, "Self-pity is of the devil, if I go off on that line I cannot be used by God for His purpose in the world."[64]

Amy Carmichael had this kind of experience of feeling of no use when she thought she was called to Ceylon, but ended up spending only a short time there. As she pondered God's purposes for that brief hiatus, she remarked, "It may be He has only sent me here as a stop gap. Part of a soldier's duty is to fill gaps, you know. One must be as willing to do nothing, as something."[65]

Oswald Chambers counsels wisely, "Notice God's unutterable waste of saints, according to the judgment of the world. God plants His saints in the most useless of places. We say—God intends me to be here because I am so useful. Jesus never estimated His life along the line of the greatest use.[66] Again he writes, "Where they will glorify Him is where God puts His saints, and we are no judge at all of where that is."[67]

## WHEN YOU FEEL UNSUCCESSFUL

Oswald Chambers stresses seeking to be faithful rather than successful, for in so doing faithfulness will result in real lasting success: "We are not called to be successful in accordance with ordinary standards, but in accordance with a corn of wheat falling into the ground and dying, becoming in that way what it never could be if it were to abide alone."[68]

Bob Buford, in his book *Halftime: Changing Your Game Plan from Success to Significance*, observes that the first part of our life we tend to be striving for success. He suggests making a "halftime" analysis of our life and focusing instead on finding significance rather than success, advising, "To make the second half better than the first, you need to discover the real you. For much of the first half, you had to be someone else."[69]

Robert Schuller points out the need for change and growth before we can be used effectively by God:

> The self-centered person has
> to grow in unselfishness
> before God says, "GO."
>
> The cautious person must
> grow in courage
> before God will say, "GO."
>
> The reckless person must
> grow in carefulness
> before God will say, "GO."
>
> The timid person must
> grow in confidence
> before God will say, "GO."
>
> The self-belittling person must
> grow in self-love
> before God will say, "GO."

The dominating person must
grow in sensitivity
before God will say, "GO."

The critical person must
grow in tolerance
before God will say, "GO."

The negative person must
grow in positive attitude
before God will say, "GO."

The power-hungry person must
grow in kindness and gentleness
before God will say, "GO."

The pleasure-seeking person must
grow in compassion for suffering people
before God will say, "GO."

And the God-ignoring soul must
become a God-adoring soul
before God will say, "GO."[70]

## TO BECOME PREPARED

The times of restlessness, uselessness, and unsuccessfulness may be times of preparation in which God is at work imperceptibly. God's purposes may be hidden to our eyes. During several of those periods of time in my life, God was still at work in my life even though I did not understand. Oswald Chambers counsels, "Remember that where you are, you are put there by God; and by the reaction of your life on the circumstances around you, you will fulfil God's purpose, as long as you keep in the light as God is in the light."[71]

The Apostle Paul was called to be an apostle at his conversion, but did not enter into apostolic ministry until 14-17 years later. Mother Teresa had to wait many years before she could establish her vision for the Missionaries of Charity. She continued to serve for many years, working together with other nuns and educating young women. Who were the first Missionaries of Charity?—The young women she trained. Her ministry was right in front of her the whole time.

## KEEP AN OPEN EYE

Faithfully serving where you are does not mean just passively accepting your circumstances and doing nothing to further your vision. You can be content serving where you are, while at the same time seeking opportunities to work toward fulfilling God's future purposes for your life. Ecclesiastes 11:1 exhorts us to cast our bread on the waters. While continuing to faithfully serve where you are, you can test the waters. Check out possibilities. Research your area of interest. Talk with others.

A friend of mine was an on-call hospice chaplain. Although she was fulfilling a much needed role, she did not feel that it best used her abilities nor was it her niche. While continuing to work in that capacity, she began to explore other possibilities. She found a whole new ministry emerging for workplace chaplains, who would provide counseling and pastoral care services for secular corporations in a variety of ways helping their employees cope through the crises of their lives—grief caregiving, career consultant, marriage, family, and divorce counseling, etc. Though this job was not her ultimate niche, it filled a need both in her life and the lives of others for a period of time.

One of my students, after graduating from college with a bachelor degree in Biblical Literature, could not find a position in ministry, so someone suggested that he do some substitute teaching for some income. The public high school principal was impressed with his work with students and took a closer look at his resume. When the principal saw that he had studied Greek and Hebrew, he figured that if he could master those languages, he could teach English and reading skills. So he hired him as a reading and English teacher and tutor, even though his degree was not in that field. As a result, he went on to obtain a Masters degree in Education with an emphasis on reading. And, in the meantime, his grandfather retired from the pastorate, so he was asked to pastor the church. Now he is finding that God has a dual calling for his life involving both pastoral ministry and education.

God's route may seem circuitous and appear to defy human reason. He took the Israelites through the wilderness, not the most direct route. We may not understand God's ways and methods, but if we are alert and available and faithful, He will make a way beyond our imaginings.

## Recognize God's Stages in Fulfilling Your Calling

*"Whenever the cloud lifted from above the Tent, the Israelites set out; wherever the cloud settled, the Israelites encamped. At the Lord's command, the Israelites set out, and at his command they encamped. As long as the cloud stayed over the tabernacle, they remained in camp"*
(Numbers 9:17-18).

What God has you doing now may not ultimately be His place for you, but it is His place for you now. To be anywhere else, or to desire being anywhere else may be out of His present will for you. God has a purpose right where you are. Solomon wrote, "There is an appointed time for everything. And there is a time for every event under heaven" (Ecclesiastes 3:1, NASB).

Perhaps you are experiencing a mid-life crisis or seeking a career change. It is good to recognize that God has different stages or purposes in His calling for our life. Career counselor John Bradley identifies five phases of career development and change: passionate pursuit of youthful dreams and goals (ages 20-30), reevaluation leading to change or redoubling efforts (early 30s), confirmation of direction or collision with mis-direction (age 35-45), accelerated performance or devastation (45-55), heightened performance or bitterness (50s and beyond).[72] It does not matter where you find yourself in one of these phases—God is at work.

A friend of mine was in mid-life seeking God's will. He had been discipled in a ministry as a young man and served on a church staff, eventually becoming pastor of the church. After several successful years in ministry, he burned out and left the ministry. He pursued schooling in another field and became a physical trainer for the Tampa Bay Buccaneers. Seeking God's will further, he went back to school again to receive a Masters degree in Counseling. While pursuing his studies, he began to work with the U.S. Department of Human Services, mentoring fathers of troubled teens. Finally, at about the age of fifty, he found his niche as a prison chaplain.

Through the years, I have been a youth worker, a furniture salesman, a jewelry salesman, a radio advertising representative, an associate pastor, a pastor, a Christian school administrator, a writer, an editor, a professor, a university administrator, a seminar Bible teacher, among other things. God has had a purpose and a plan for my life in each one of these arenas.

I have found through the years that each situation I have been in has been a preparation for what God intended to do in me and through me down the road. For instance, I mentioned earlier how a tradition delivering children's sermon prepared me for becoming a Christian school administrator and being an effective communicator with children.

That in turn led me to serving as a Christian school administrator in another church and opening up opportunities to utilize my teaching gifts in greater ways. Also that church had a vision for a Bible college, so I laid out plans and curriculum to establish a college. While the leadership lost the vision for the school due to a church split, the desire and plans were still in my heart. I experienced death of a vision. Yet several years later that led to a unique position as a university administrator and professor, helping local churches set up their own Bible institutes in joint relationship with the university. It fit like a hand in a glove!

God works in stages in our lives. He leads us to set out, then to settle down. Then he lifts the cloud of the anointing of His Spirit, and leads us to another assignment.

As long as we are obedient to His command and sensitive to the promptings of His Holy Spirit, we will remain in the purposes of God. Some are too settled and not desirous of change. If you are too comfortable and want to maintain the status quo, the Lord may be saying it is time to pick up your tent and move camp. The cloud of God may be moving and you need to move with it.

Or you may want to move on, yet the Lord is saying, "Stay a while longer." If where you are now seems to be a wilderness, a place of exile, a situation from which you want to escape, God may be saying to you as He did to the people in exile in Babylon in Jeremiah's day, "Build houses and settle down; plant gardens and eat what they produce. . . . Also, seek the peace and prosperity of the city. . . because if it prospers, you too will prosper" (Jeremiah 29:5, 7). Build, bear fruit, enjoy life, seek the welfare of others where you are, pray for others. Find your fulfillment in your present situation. Keep on keeping on until God opens another door.

## YOU ARE NEVER TOO OLD OR TOO YOUNG!

You may be thinking, "I am too young or too old to launch out in my dream." On the contrary, no one is too old or too young. God's purposes are fulfilled in our lives regardless of our age.

Paul told Timothy, "Let no one despise your youth." The Lord told Jeremiah, "Do not say, 'I am only a child.' You must go to everyone I send you to and say whatever I command you. Do not be afraid of them, for I am with you and will rescue you" (Jeremiah 1:7-8). God used Joan of Arc as a teenager. Children sometimes were anointed to preach and minister in the great Indonesian revival of the 1960s. Many of the great inventors and musicians began as a child. Mozart wrote one of his great pieces of music as a teenager. Charles Spurgeon began pastoring as a teenager. Known as "the child evangelist," a twelve-year old girl by the name of Uldine Utley preached to crowds of thousands in many places around the United States, including Madison Square Garden.

Never think that you are too old either. John MacMillan was a Canadian businessman with a printing business—a Presbyterian layman and elder who as a young man desired to become a missionary to China. But because of family and business responsibilities, he was unable to go. So he began to work with Jewish and Chinese people in his hometown of Toronto. Then he met a former missionary to China who had worked with Hudson Taylor and China Inland Mission, but had to return to Canada because of health problems. They married and together continued to work with the Chinese in Toronto. His desire was being fulfilled in ways he did not imagine. And then, at the age of 49, John MacMillan and his wife were asked to take over the publication work of The Christian and Missionary Alliance in South China. He became ordained on the mission field, and later became the Field Director of the mission in the Philippines, then a college professor and magazine editor. For more than 30 years, until he died in his 80s, he was actively used by God, especially in spiritual warfare ministry.

Even if you are in your 50s or 60s or 70s or even 80s, God may have a great ministry for you. One of the greatest ministries for retired people or the elderly is intercession. As a pastor, my greatest prayer warriors were often people in their 70s and 80s. One of my mentors in his 70s became physically unable to live alone, but continued to witness, lead Bible studies and disciple both residents and employees of the nursing home where he stayed. He led a seniors' Sunday School class up until a month before he died.

When I was studying Hebrew in college, two of my classmates were women in their 70s. They wanted to do ministry among Jewish people. One of my colleagues who completed his Doctor of Ministry degree at the same time as I did was a 68 year old former Roman Catholic priest who had married late in life and had a 13 year old son. He wrote his doctoral dissertation on the youth ministry he had started. After completing his degree, he became a pastor in the Foursquare Church denomination.

You are never too old or too young to be used by God. As long or as short as you live, God has a purpose for your life.

## LET YOUR NICHE FIND YOU

*The Lord said to [Moses], "What is that in your hand?" And he said, "A staff." Then He said, "Throw it on the ground." So he threw it on the ground, and it became a serpent; and Moses fled from it. Then the Lord said to Moses, "Stretch out your hand and grasp it by the tail."—so he stretched out his hand and caught it, and it became a staff in his hand. . . . Moses took the staff of God in his hand"*
(Exodus 4:2-4, 20, NASB).

Sometimes, rather than finding your niche, your niche will find you. If you offer to God what is in your hand, He will transform it and use it for His purposes, just as Moses' staff became the staff of God. How do we cooperate with God's purposes to let our niche find us?

### *Do What You Already Know to Do*

My sister Shirley enjoyed a hobby of wood-burning pictures on boxes and plaques. She worked diligently at crafting simple pieces, then taking on more challenging sketches. Initially, she began giving some of her handiwork as gifts. Eventually became so good at it that people asked if she could make something for them to give to someone else. She began selling her work, and it has become a good source of supplementary income. Her niche found her in doing what she likes to do and doing it well.

I mentioned earlier, a friend of mine was graduating from seminary and we talked about planting a church together. He had been in social work and needed a new job to provide an income for his family while working toward planting a church, so he found employment working as a prison chaplain. However, the work became so consuming that he did not have time to do church planting (to my disappointment—death of a vision). Nonetheless, his chaplaincy work became his ministry. His niche found him, not in planting a church, but in ministering to what he called "the church in chains"—a new vision God had given him. He now works as a chaplain with federal prisons, and has had opportunity to minister in prisons in other countries as well.

## Be Diligent and Faithful

If you will be diligent and faithful in doing the thing God puts before you, God will open up His niche for your life. Solomon repeatedly observed this principle:

"A man's gift makes room for him
And brings him before great men" (Proverbs 18:16, NASB).

"The plans of the diligent lead surely to advantage,
But everyone who is hasty comes surely to poverty"
(Proverbs 21:5, NASB).

"Do you see a man skilled in his work? He will stand before kings; he will not stand before obscure men"
(Proverbs 22:29, NASB).

## Be Sensitive and Obedient to the Leadings of the Spirit

*"Cast your bread upon the waters, for after many days you will find it again"* (Ecclesiastes 11:1).

When I was serving as a pastor several years ago, I had an urge, almost an obsession, to study in-depth a certain theological issue that affected my congregation, as well as those to whom I ministered outside the congregation. So I researched and wrote down my thoughts and ideas. I put together a paper for the beginnings of an article or book and sent it to a publisher. He was not interested in it, but encouraged me to write something else somewhat related to the original topic. So I wrote another article, which he accepted for publication in a journal. Not long after that, he told me he liked my work, and he was particularly interested in a *footnote* I had written on the concept of binding and loosing in Matthew 16:19. He commented that he had been wanting to write a book on the concept and asked if I would be interested in co-authoring the book with him. That obscure little paragraph led to my first book publication, which then led to another book authored by myself and published by the same publisher.

That original urging of the Holy Spirit to research and write mushroomed into a much broader writing and speaking ministry. If I had neglected or questioned that urging, doubting whether it would be worth the effort, the desired directions of the Lord for my life would not have been put in motion and opportunities would have been lost.

## *Do What Is Before You with All Your Might*

We will never find our niche with a half-hearted effort. We must not give in to complacency, mediocrity, lethargy, or depression. Again to quote Solomon's wisdom, "whatever your hand finds to do, do it with all your might" (Ecclesiastes 9:10, NASB). When you do this, God will open up new doors for you.

In Exodus 4, God asked Moses, "What is that in your hand?" He replied, "A staff." He threw it down and it became a serpent. Then God told him to pick it up, and it became a staff once again. However, it was not the same staff. Later in the chapter, the text says that "Moses took up the staff of God." It was no longer the staff of Moses, but the staff of God. He used that staff to perform miracles and cross the Red Sea. If we will offer before the Lord what is in our hand, no matter how insignificant it may seem, God can transform it for His purposes. That which is ordinary becomes extraordinary. Use what is in your hand and God will make use of you.

## *Be Content in Your Niche*

Some people have found their niche but they are still not satisfied. They are still looking for something more, something bigger. We need to be happy in the niche where God has placed us. Don't try to be someone else. Don't try to imitate another person's success. The Apostle Paul exhorted every person to stay in his or her assignment (1 Corinthians 7:20). Your niche is your assignment from the Lord.

## *Don't Grow Weary*

Paul exhorts us, "A man reaps what he sows. . . . The one who sows to please the Spirit, from the Spirit will reap eternal life. Let us not become weary in doing good, for at the proper time we will reap a harvest if we do not give up. Therefore, as we have opportunity, let us do good to all people, especially to those who belong to the family of believers." (Galatians 6:7-9). How do we not grow weary? How do we not give up? We can do the following:

*Keep serving.* Keep on keeping on. Maintain a servant spirit. Continue deeds of kindness and compassion. Give of yourself out of your heart, not out of duty. Don't quit. Don't give up.

*Keep cultivating.* Keep sowing the seed. Plow up the soil. Fertilize the soil. Water the soil. Weed the garden. Make sure what you are sowing and nurturing gets enough heat and light.

*Take Sabbath breaks.* We often grow weary because we have ignored the Sabbath principle in Scripture. God built us to reserve one third of our day and one seventh of our week for rest. If we ignore God's design, we will break down.

*Don't lose hope.* Solomon warned "Hope deferred makes the heart sick." (Proverbs 13:12).

*Abide in Christ.* Keep being nourished by communion with God and meditation of His Word. If you are abiding in the vine of the presence of the Lord, His energizing strength will flow into you to overcome any weariness of soul or body.

*Keep your armor on.* Daniel prophesied regarding the antichrist spirit, "He shall speak great words against the most High, and shall wear out the saints of the most High" (Daniel 7:25, KJV). The devil loves to wear down believers. If he can find a space where we have not kept the armor of God on, or find a chink in that armor, he will exploit our weaknesses to the max.

*Keep standing.* "Having done all, stand firm." (Ephesians 6:10). "He who endures to the end shall be saved." The implication of these words is that we can, by the power of Christ, stand firm. We can endure. It is a matter of taking our stand, and sticking with it.

Ultimately, we have the promise of God's Word, "Faithful is He who calls you and He also will bring it to pass" (1 Thessalonians 5:24, NASB). If He has called us, He will bring us through and open the doors, if only we will not grow weary.

## FOR FURTHER REFLECTION

1. Who are the people closest to you? How can you minister to their needs?

2. What needs can you fill in your local church?

3. What are the needs of your co-workers, neighbors, or school mates? How can you minister to their needs?

4. What other people do you know who have needs? How can you minister to them?

5. Are you aware of any other "divine encounters" God may have arranged in His purposes for your life?

6. What is the status of your present situation? What might be God's purposes in your present circumstances?

7. How can you be faithful where you are?

8. What might God be doing in your life now? What is He wanting to change in your life? What character qualities does He desire to develop? How is He honing or refining your life?

9. What stages has God taken you through in His purposes and in preparing you for the next stages of His purposes?

10. What stage of God's purposes are you in now, and how did God prepare you?

11. What do you think is the next stage in God's purposes for your life and how are you being prepared?

12. What ordinary thing in your hand might God want to use?

13. Is there something you have not persevered in doing, something that you have neglected or given up on, that the Lord might want to use in your life?

14. How can God transform the ordinary things of your life?

15. What do you need to put your full effort into with diligence and faithfulness?

# Discover God's Purposes in Your Trials

## GOD'S WAYS IN WILDERNESS WANDERINGS

I thought I went through my midlife crisis early at the age of about 30. When I turned forty years old, I thought that now that I had finished my forty years in the wilderness, I was poised to enter the Promised Land. But then someone reminded me that it was Moses' second forty years he spent in the deserts of the Sinai peninsula. Maybe my wilderness was still ahead of me! Indeed, there were times in the next several years that it really seemed so. By the time I turned 45 I believed I was just treading water and making no progress, and never would. But within three months God turned my life around and I began to enter my Promised Land.

## ANOTHER LAP AROUND MOUNT SINAI

Sometimes we feel like we are going nowhere in our lives. We seem to be wandering aimlessly in the wilderness like the Israelites after leaving Egypt. Or it may appear like we are going in circles, going over the same ground again and again. We say, "I've been here before. I've been there and done that." Or we pray, "Lord, I thought I learned that lesson, so why am I here again in the same place facing the same problem?" In the words of a Keith Green song, we "take another lap around Mount Sinai."

It is true that if we don't learn our lessons the first time, we may have to tread the same ground again until we get it right. Sometimes ten years of experience may be one year of experience repeated ten times. I have had lessons I thought I had learned, but made the same mistake again. So the first thing that we need to do is to recognize that mistake, repent of it, correct it, and determine not to go that way again. The Israelites show us that even when God works miraculously in our lives, we easily forget what He has done and where He brought us from. So we often need to go through painful reminders—goads that get us back on track.

To use another familiar example for those who fly, sometimes the airplane keeps circling above the airport for a long period of time waiting for clearance to land. Similarly, sometimes it seems like we just keep circling and circling without landing. But God knows when it is clear, when is the proper and best time, when it is your time, just as the tower knows when the runway is ready, when it is clear for your plane to land. When you don't get clearance, you run the risk of getting on the wrong runway or colliding with another plane. You put yourself in a danger zone.

## GOD'S PLAN FOR THE WILDERNESS

God did plan for the Israelites to spend some time in the wilderness—about two years, in order to prepare them for the battles of Canaan—boot camp, so to speak. God was training them physically for the rigors and disciplines needed for warfare. He was building community and teamwork and the principle of operating under authority. He was teaching them to trust in Him and His supernatural intervention and provision. Your wilderness may be a spiritual boot camp for greater ministry and spiritual warfare.

After exploring the deserts of the Sinai Peninsula and tracing the journey of the Israelites, Jamie Buckingham wrote about the spiritual insights he gleaned from his experiences:

> God did something that still mystifies mortal man: He began the process of spiritual education by thrusting Moses into the great and terrible wilderness of Sinai. Here he learned to distinguish between passion and principle, between impulse and settled purpose. Only in the wilderness does one learn that mere need never constitutes a call. One learns to wait on the voice of God. . . .
>
> These were years in which his rough edges were sanded smooth. The literal blast furnace of the Sinai refined the character of a man God was going to use. There he learned to pray and he learned the values of solitude. There, starting with a few sheep and goats, he learned the principles of leadership.[73]

In Deuteronomy 8 God reveals His purposes in the midst of the desert experiences and dry times of our lives. We can find at least seven purposes in this chapter:

- To humble us (verses 2, 16)
- To test and prove us (verses 2, 16)
- To reveal what is in our heart (verse 2)—self-discovery
- To reconsider and realign our priorities (verse 3) ("Man does not live by bread alone")
- To become disciplined (verse 5)—developing endurance and spiritual stamina
- To learn to trust God for supernatural provision and protection (verses 4, 15, 16)
- To cause us to be grateful (verses 11-14)
- To give God praise, recognition and glory (verses 17-18)

These insights, among many others, show us that God has vital intentions he wants to accomplish in our seeming times of purposelessness. Buckingham comments, "Thus the wilderness remains a place of purification and preparation—a place where a man can learn to distinguish between the clamoring voices of this world and the often quiet, gentle voice of God. . . . To bypass the wilderness in our journey to the Promised Land is to bypass God."[74]

However, sometimes we extend our time in the wilderness much longer than God intended. Because of unbelief and disobedience the Israelites spent forty years in the wilderness. When we do not act in faith, we fail to obey fully God's commands. God does not condemn us, but it takes longer to get back on the track of His purposes for our life.

## GOING IN CIRCLES OR SPIRALS?

But at other times, the Lord may be doing something else. There are times that when it seems like we are going in circles, in spite of the fact we have trusted the Lord and have been obedient to him. There is no big sin in our life keeping us from moving on. So God is at work even in those times. I discovered this once when I was in one of those recurring cycles and sought the Lord about it. He showed me that I was not going in circles, but in *spirals*. To me, it seemed like I was just going round and round, not going anywhere, but from God's perspective, when I was going around again, it was at a new plane. Each time I went around, it was at a higher level than before. Like climbing a steep mountain you may go around and around the mountain as you go higher or go through several switchbacks.

So when it appears we are going nowhere, in reality, we are progressing spiritually—learning lessons at a higher dimension, gaining victory on a higher plane—moving progressively upward and onward. As C. S. Lewis depicted in his book *The Last Battle* in the series *The Chronicles of Narnia*, we go "further up and further in."

If we have had cycles of defeat within our lives, we need to go back over those areas to develop cycles of victory. We need to replace the negative patterns and habits with godly patterns and habits. Like the process of memorization, repeating such actions within in our lives reinforces and indelibly imprints the divine changes God is making in our life.

If you were to do a study of all of the places the Israelites stopped in their wilderness wanderings, you would see that, though they appeared aimless to the Israelite people, God had a purpose to accomplish at each one. Those who cooperated with God's purposes made it into the Promised Land. God's ways are not our ways, and God's route is often circuitous. God's way is not always the shortest distance between two points. But God's way is good and will ultimately accomplish His greater purposes.

Two weeks after I had moved my family a thousand miles to take a new job, my wife's brother suddenly died. In addition to the trauma and depression that followed, she did not like the community to which we had moved and became homesick for her family. We agonized during that period of time. We found great encouragement and hope in a Hebrew chorus we learned in our new church:

✺ He did not bring us out this far to take us back again,
He brought us out to bring us in to the Promised Land.
Though there be giants in that land, we need not be afraid.
He brought us out to bring us in to the Promised Land.[75]

No matter what wilderness you are going through in your life, there is a Promised Land for your life. There is a way through. There is a light at the end of the tunnel. Continue to persevere. As Jesus encouraged, "He who endures to the end shall be saved (healed, restored, renewed)." God promises He will make a way in the wilderness:

Behold, I will do something new,
Now it will spring forth;
Will you not be aware of it?
I will even make a roadway in the wilderness,
Rivers in the desert. (Isaiah 43:19, NASB).

What seems like a waste in our lives—a waste of time, energy, talent, God will bless. Nothing is a waste in God's economy as long as we have an attitude of gratitude and obedience.

## Surviving Our Wildernesses

How do we make it through our wilderness experiences? First of all, we trust God to supply our needs and to lead us through. God has not left us alone, even though sometimes it may seem He is not present. In Deuteronomy 8 Moses recounted the provision and direction of God throughout the years of wilderness wandering of the Israelites:

"He led you though the great and terrible wilderness . . ."
(verse 15a)
"He brought water for you out of the rock of flint . . ."
(verse 15b)
"He fed you manna . . ." (verse 16)

Like Moses, we need to remember and recite with gratitude the things that God has done.

Secondly, we need to realize that the dry periods are seasonal and temporary, not a permanent state. The interesting thing about rivers in the wilderness of Sinai and the Negev desert in the southern part of Israel is that they only run in seasons. Many times during the year the riverbeds, called wadis, are dry. It is only when the spring and autumn rains come, or when the snow melts off the mountains, that the rivers gush forth with water, and then they often come in torrents. In our lives, there will be times in which we feel parched. But we can anticipate that the floodwaters are coming in due season. David uses another image: "Weeping may last for the night, but a shout of joy comes in the morning." (Psalm 30:5b, NASB).

In the meantime, we can search for water. Yes, there is water in the desert, but you have to search for it. Look for little signs of life in your wilderness, mini-oases where you can refresh yourself. Oftentimes in the wadis the gushing waters in the rainy seasons carve out holes in the rocks that hold water, hidden from view. You need to look for hidden springs and reservoirs, and dig deep. Sometimes even in the dry seasons, plants can be seen along the dry riverbed clinging to the channel for life, reaching their roots deep to soak up what little nourishment it can find until the waters gush forth once again. So we need to send our roots deep into our relationship and fellowship with God and cling to the promises of God and the expectant hope that he will see us through.

Then we need to partake of the daily manna provided by God. This nourishment comes through the disciplines of prayer, study of the Word of God, meditation and praise. Sometimes these practices become routines for us, but they are needed routines to sustain us through the dry times. When the Israelites first received manna, they were excited about the new sweet delight. But after eating the same thing over and over again, day in and day out, they tired of it. Yet it was God's supernatural provision. Even if our devotional life seems to be the "same old same old," yet it is still God's provision for our daily nourishment.

Finally, when the floods come, we need to harness the floods. The modern Israelis have learned to channel the floodwaters to provide reservoirs and to irrigate crops, so that the deserts have blossomed with life. Likewise, we need to channel the life of the Spirit within our life so that when the dry seasons come, we do not become empty, but have the channel of the life of the Spirit still flowing in our life.

## GREAT NEWS—YOU ARE DESTINED FOR TRIALS!

*"We sent Timothy, our brother and God's fellow-worker in the gospel*
*of Christ, to strengthen and encourage you as to your faith; so that no*
*man may be disturbed by these afflictions; for you yourselves know*
*that we have been destined for this"*
(1 Thessalonians 3:2-3, NASB).

Paul tells us in this Scripture that we are destined for trials or afflictions (the Greek word means pressures or stress). The Greek word for destiny in this verse can even mean *appointed*. Trials are a part of our destiny. We have an appointment with pressure. But don't despair. Lamentations 3:32-33 assures us, "Though he brings grief, he will show compassion, so great is his unfailing love. For he does not willingly bring affliction or grief to the children of men." God will spare us any affliction that we do not need. Yet He knows that it is often only through suffering that He can work His character and His ways in our lives. As

*[handwritten margin note: Suffering is a part of our destiny because of the fallen state of the world, not because of God.]*

— *128* —

Paul affirmed, "We also exult in our tribulations; knowing that tribulation brings about perseverance; and perseverance, proven character; and proven character, hope" (Romans 5:3-4, NASB).

Paul Billheimer, in his book *Don't Waste Your Sorrows*, explains, "Because tribulation is necessary for the decentralization of self and the development of deep dimensions of *agape* love, this love can only be developed in the school of suffering. . . . There is no sainthood without suffering."[76] God is more concerned about our character than our ministry. In his book *Adventure in Adversity*, Billheimer has also declared, "When a saint is passing through a heavy trial, God is aiming at twice as much as before."[77]

*Disagree*

Billheimer sees three purposes of God for every believer in the afflictions of Job:

- A new vision of God
- A deeper death to the natural self-life
- Enlargement of the sufferer's prosperity

Which of these purposes may God be seeking to accomplish in your life through your trials?

## WHEN OTHERS THWART OUR PLANS

Why does God allow injustice? Joseph was a godly young man who had shown himself faithful in prison and had been promoted from slavery to become a steward—a servant in charge of Potiphar's household. Then Potiphar's wife tried to seduce him. He resisted her advances and fled the scene—a godly, biblical response. But look where it got him. Falsely accused of attempted rape, he was put back in prison—through no fault of his own. We do not understand God's ways—why he had to be incarcerated for doing what was right—but we do know that God used the situation to work out His plan in His timing. "You meant evil against me, but God meant it for good" (Genesis 50:20, NASB).

We must be willing to forgive others, or we will be stuck in our past. If we keep looking back, like Lot's wife we become frozen like a pillar of salt. God's plans cannot ultimately be thwarted by others if we are walking in obedience to Him. But if we refuse to forgive, we thwart ourselves as well.

Job was a godly man, yet God allowed him to be attacked viciously by Satan. Job had many questions and complaints, but did you ever realize that when God finally did respond, He never answered Job's questions. God will never answer all of our questions, but He will turn the situation around for good. One of my mentors, Dr. Chuck Farah, made a statement I will never forget: "Maturity is to understand that we don't need to understand." If we are growing deep in Christ, we will have an implicit trust in Him that nothing can shake, and we don't need to ask "why?" We don't need to understand.

Paul confessed, "Satan thwarted us" (1 Thessalonians 2:18, NASB). After many years of ministry he recognized that hindrances will come again and again. He wrote to the church at Corinth, "For a wide door for effective service has opened to me, and there are many adversaries" (1 Corinthians 16:9, NASB).

We have a choice. We can continue to seethe and rail about the injustice and unfairness done to us, and go nowhere, or we can choose not to remain bitter, not to let that person or persons continue to derail our future by our attitude. We can determine to be incensed no longer, but to pick ourselves back up, dust ourselves off, and go again in a new direction. God is not surprised when others do us wrong or block a doorway. He will always make a way, and His way is better. No other person can prevent God's will from being done in your life if you walk in faith and obedience to Him.

## Disappointments, Failures, and Death of a Vision

Even in your disappointments and failures God has a purpose. An ancient maxim proclaims, "God's delays are not God's denials." As I have mentioned, in past years, two opportunities for advancements and promotion opened up to be almost certainties, only to be slammed shut. I was greatly disappointed, even depressed for a period of time. In both situations, I felt like the rug had been pulled out from under me—a carrot dangled in front of me, only to be held out of reach. Unjust opposition and interference from others and mistaken responses and lack of savvy on my part contributed to the reversals of the opportunities.

Yet God had other purposes for my life, and He has since blessed me in many other ways. God opened other doors, and also expanded the opportunities for ministry in my existing situation. Sometimes one open door will lead to another, or even a closed door may divert us to find an open door in another direction. In his book *A Way Through the Wilderness*, Jamie Buckingham avowed, "God never brings a hindrance into our lives that He does not intend to be used to open another door that would not have been opened otherwise."[78]

Bill Gothard, in his Institute in Basic Life Principles, talks about the biblical principle of "death of a vision." God gives us a vision, then allows it to die, so that He can resurrect it and fulfill it supernaturally beyond human imagination and effort. God gave Abraham a vision of generations of descendents to follow him. But, alas, Sarah became too old to conceive and God had not done anything—*Death of a vision*. So Sarah and Abraham try to help God out and fulfill the vision through their own ideas and efforts—and it results in Ishmael. God says, "No, he is not the fulfillment"—*Double death of a vision*. Then God supernaturally enables Sarah to conceive, and Isaac is born to fulfill the vision. But then God instructs Abraham to sacrifice Isaac—*Triple death of a vision!* Finally, God provides the ram as the provision for the sacrifice and the vision is once again resurrected and ultimately fulfilled.

Joseph had a dream of being in a place of authority with his parents and brothers bowing down to him. When he shared his vision with his family, perhaps out of youthful braggadocio, he was rejected by his brothers and sold into slavery—*Death of a vision*. He worked faithfully as a slave and was promoted to a place of authority as steward over Potiphar's household, seemingly a fulfillment of his vision. But then his master's wife tries to seduce him and he responds in godly fashion, fleeing temptation. Yet he is falsely accused of attempted rape and put in prison—*Double death of a vision*. He worked faithfully in prison, and met the Pharaoh's butler and cupbearer, enabled supernaturally from God to interpret their dreams. He gains hope as he asks the cupbearer to speak to Pharaoh about the injustice done him, but the cupbearer forgets him—*Triple death of a vision!* Finally, when Pharaoh is troubled by dreams no one can interpret, the cupbearer remembers Joseph, and he is called to Pharaoh. He interprets Pharaoh's dream and is promoted from prison to prince hood as the second in authority over the kingdom of Egypt. Eventually, his family does bow down to him, fulfilling the dream of a dozen years earlier, after death of the vision three times.

God often does this in our lives as well. He gives us a vision, a dream, a desire. Then something comes along to squash that vision. We hold onto God, seek His face, and eventually the vision is fulfilled, sometimes after the second or third death of the vision, just as God did with my dream to obtain a doctorate. God's ways and thoughts are not our ways and thoughts. He fulfills His vision for our life in His own ways, which we do not understand. In that way, He gets the glory for its fulfillment, not our efforts.

## GOD'S WILL FOR YOU—THE NOBLEST PART!

There is an old poem that God has used to speak to me again and again in my periods of trials and wilderness experiences. Let these words speak to your heart:

> When God wants to drill a man
> And thrill a man
> And skill a man,
> When God wants to mold a man
> To play the noblest part;
> When He yearns with all His heart
> To create so great and bold a man
> That all the world shall be amazed
> Watch His methods, watch His ways!
> How He ruthlessly perfects
> Whom He royally elects!
> How He hammers him and hurts him,
> And with mighty blows converts him
> Into trial shapes of clay which
> Only God understands;
> While his tortured heart is crying
> And he lifts beseeching hands!
> How He bends but never breaks
> When His good He undertakes;
> How He uses whom He chooses
> And with every purpose fuses him;
> By every act induces him
> To try His splendor out –
> God knows what He's about![79]

Author Unknown

God knows what He is about in your life!

Thanks Calvin...

• I believe God is able to use "wilderness" times to teach us, but that He doesn't create them. We create them, or Satan, but faith, and corresponding action, pull us out.

## FOR FURTHER REFLECTION

1. Describe a wilderness in your life currently or in your past.

2. What has God been endeavoring to accomplish in your wilderness?

3. Are you going in a circle or a spiral? What ground do you seem to be re-treading in your life and why?

4. How can you survive your wilderness experience?

5. What trials have you gone through?

6. How has God worked His character and ways in your life?

7. What disappointments, failures or death of vision have you experienced?

8. How is God working out His purposes through all these experiences?

# Remove Hindrances to Finding Your Niche

*"Let us throw off everything that hinders and the sin that so easily entangles, and let us run with perseverance the race marked out for us"* (Hebrews 12:1).

There are at least five hindrances to finding our niche and coming to the place where God can use us effectively. First of all, our personal ambitions get in the way of want God wants. Secondly, unresolved issues from our past act as barriers to our present and future. Third, if we have somehow gotten off track and missed the will of God, until we get back on the right track, we cannot find the niche God has for us. The fourth issue is forgiveness. Either we need to obtain forgiveness and make restitution for things we have done wrong, or else we may need to forgive someone else for an offense against us. Finally, mediocrity, not giving it our best, often closes God's doors for our niche.

## SURRENDER YOUR AMBITIONS

*By faith Abraham, when God tested him, offered Isaac as a sacrifice* (Hebrews 11:17).

The Apostle Paul tells us, "Here is a trustworthy saying: If anyone sets his heart on being an overseer, he desires a noble task" (1 Timothy 3:1). Leadership is an honorable ambition. Ambitions are not wrong if they are submitted to God and channeled by the leading of the Holy Spirit. A.W. Tozer explains:

A true and safe leader is likely to be one who has no desire to lead, but is forced into a position by the inward pressure of the Holy Spirit and the press of [circumstances]. . . . The man who is ambitious to lead is disqualified as a leader. The true leader will have no desire to lord it over God's heritage, but will be humble, gentle, self-sacrificing and altogether ready to follow when the Spirit chooses another to lead.[80]

Oswald Chambers advises, "If you seek great things for yourself—'God has called me for this and that,' you are putting a barrier to God's use of you."[81] The times when I have begun to seek great things for myself are times when God has had to allow those ambitions to crumble and those visions to die. Alan Redpath counsels:

Now, I imagine that many of you have visions of some great project that you are going to do for God, but you are always planning a scheme and thinking out a method by which you can win souls to Jesus. Very good, but it is only second best. God's best is for you to die! For God has nothing else whatsoever for the most refined, educated, business man or woman, or on the other hand, for the most profligate sinner. . . . The thing that God is calling on some people to do, people who want to do big things for Him, is to die with Jesus.[82]

God can and does place ambitions within us. Yet all ambitions must be surrendered, laid at the foot of the Cross—again and again. Many years ago I had been attempting several times to work on a doctorate, but time and time again, my plans fell through. While spending some time in prayer and fasting, I read a little book by the great French archbishop Francois Fenelon entitled *Let Go*. He counseled, "So give yourself up to His plans. . . . Learn to cultivate peace. And you can do this by learning to turn a deaf ear to your own ambitious thoughts."[83]

After reading this, I surrendered my ambition to the Lord, saying, "Lord, you know I have tried several times to work on my doctorate. I thought this was Your will, but it has never worked out. I lay this on the altar before you. If you want me to get a doctorate, Lord, you will have to make it happen." Five years later I was employed by a university, and they not only wanted me to get a doctorate, but they paid for it! When I surrendered it to the Lord, he worked it out in His way and time.

Several years ago, I had anticipated a significant promotion that fell through. Again, I had to lay ambitions on the altar before the Lord. When

I yielded all my hopes and plans to Him, though I did not get the promotion, the Lord has blessed abundantly in other ways—in ministry opportunities, in fulfillment, in finances, and in many other blessings. Once we surrender our ambitions to God, He can resurrect them into something beautiful, even better. As Oswald Chambers counsels, "When I stop telling God what I want, He can catch me up for what He wants without let or hindrance."[84]

Just as we pointed out earlier, when our desires are God's desires, we find our purpose. When we submit our desires to Him, He sifts and purifies them so that they are no longer our ambitions, but His. When they are His aspirations for us, they are honorable and pure. Then we can seek great things, not for ourselves, but for God. William Carey said, "Expect great things from God. Attempt great things for God."[85]

## WRESTLE WITH YOUR PAST ISSUES

*"So Jacob was left alone, and a man wrestled with him until daybreak"* (Genesis. 32:24).

*"Forgetting those things that are behind, and reaching forward to what lies ahead"* (Phil. 3:13, NASB).

### *Facing Past Issues*

We all have a past to deal with that at some point in our life comes back to haunt us. If we have already dealt with it, then we can say with Paul, "There is now no condemnation for those who are in Christ Jesus" (Romans 8:1). Satan is the "accuser of the brethren" (Revelation 12:10), so we should recognize that he comes to attack us with our past mistakes and sins. But if we have confessed them to God and made things right, Satan has no right to accuse us. We are free from condemnation.

However, if there are sins of our past that we have not resolved or made proper restitution, the Enemy comes back to attack us in that area. Jacob may have put Laban behind him, but he was faced with his past deception and injustice to his brother Esau. If we are to go on with the Lord, and enter into His Promised Land for our lives, we will have to be confronted with our past sooner or later. God may allow our past to rise up once again in that area, but it is not for the purpose of our destruction. Rather, God puts the pressure on a sore spot in our life that needs to be worked on or put back in proper alignment.

When my wife occasionally gives me a back rub down, she sometimes hits a nerve and I jump or cringe in pain. That indicates a tender location that needs attention and needs additional pressure applied to it to work out the soreness in the muscle. A similar thing happens in our lives spiritually, when God puts His finger on a nerve, a sore spot in our lives that needs attention and changing. Our natural reaction is to recoil and wriggle away from painful touch.

Just as Jacob had run away from his conflict with his brother Esau many years earlier, so we have a tendency to turn away from, or avoid, or hide our conflicts. We get along fairly well in our life, making a life for ourselves like Jacob, but never dealing with the original problem.

But if we are to move on in God and His purposes and will for our life and come into our inheritance spiritually, we have to come face to face with those areas of our life we have been avoiding all these years. If we are to mature in Christ, to live the victorious Christian life, to receive our Promised Land, we have to be confronted with our Esaus. So often we obey God by the front door and retreat by the back door. We leave ourselves an exit. But at some point, like Jacob leaving Laban, God causes our bridges to be burnt behind us, locks the back door and puts on the squeeze so that we are backed into a corner or between a rock and a hard place.

We want to find God's purpose in our life—unless it means dealing with past issues. We want to lead without being led. We want authority without being under authority. We want to be spiritual, but we don't want to be made spiritual. We want progress if we can have it without change. God wants to change us. But most of us are willing to change, not when we see the light, but when we feel the heat. God will do whatever it takes to make of us a man or woman of God. An old poem says He is the hound of Heaven.

To become mature we must be flexible, adaptable, moveable, and bendable. In order to get to that place, we need to experience confrontation, just as Jacob was confronted with his brother and the possibility of the consequences of revenge for Jacob's deception (Genesis 32:6-7). When God wants us to move on in Him, the first thing He does is confront us with something displeasing to Him, some roadblock to spiritual maturity. We are faced with our past, something left unresolved. Perhaps it is something we see as a strength, not a weakness or outright evil. Watchman Nee has observed, "As long as we live, our natural strength pursues us. It is always being dealt with by God."

Next, we might sense abandonment. In Genesis 32:24 Jacob was left alone. When God is dealing with us He gets us alone. We feel abandoned—even by God. We feel as if no one understands—wife, husband, friend, church, pastor. Richard Foster describes this as the "Prayer of the Forsaken" or the "Sahara of the heart" in his classic book *Prayer: Finding the Heart's True Home.*[86]

## GOD'S PRESSURE POINTS

After confronting us with our past, then God struggles with us (v. 24). We thought our struggle was with Satan, but in reality it is with the messenger of the Lord. Jacob and the angel wrestled until daybreak. God will wrestle through with us until the light comes and the issue is resolved. It is what the old saints like John of the Cross called the long dark night of the soul.

Sometimes we do not recognize the thing we wrestle with is God— that irritation in our life, that pain in the neck, that thing that is grating on us. We may blame our spouse, circumstances, children, boss, co-worker, church, but the real issue is the attitude, habit or action God is trying to change in our lives. We may complain that we are being pressured or stressed out. What we resist or feel pressure in is usually where God is dealing with us.

There are several ways we may respond to pressure and conflict. We may try to avoid it or run away from it. We try to evade the issue, or try to hide from God as Adam after he ate of the forbidden fruit. We may resist pressure and get relief. We are inclined to try to lessen the pressure on ourselves by putting pressure on someone else. When God is dealing with a husband, for instance, he may put pressure on his wife and children. We release the pressure by blowing off steam or blaming someone else or our problems. Or we may give into pressure by succumbing or giving up. We end in defeat.

Or we can do as Jacob did, and wrestle with the pressure (v. 25). There can be healthy tension in pressure. Isometric pressure builds muscles. The purpose of pressure is to form character, to build spiritual muscles. Paul asserted, "Through many tribulations we must enter the kingdom of God." (Acts 14:22, NASB). The Greek word for tribulation means "pressure." Paul assured us that our tribulations [pressures] can produce perseverance and proven character (Romans 5:3-4). As mentioned in Chapter 3, diamonds are formed from dead, decaying plants under time, heat, and pressure—which forms coal—and then through more time, heat and pressure becomes diamonds. God uses the pressures of our life to form us into beautiful diamonds.

If God is not dealing with some area of your life and applying pressure, that may mean that you are spiritually anemic and ineffective, that you are not moving on in God.

Annie Johnson Flint, in her poem "Pressed," aptly expresses the work of God through the pressures of our life:

> Pressed out of measure and pressed to all length;
> Pressed so intensely it seems beyond strength.
> Pressed in the body and pressed in the soul;
> Pressed in the mind till the dark surges roll;
> Pressure by foes, and pressure by friends;
> Pressure on pressure, till life nearly ends.
> Pressed into loving the staff and the rod;
> Pressed into knowing no helper but God.
> Pressed into liberty where nothing clings;
> Pressed into faith for impossible things.
> Pressed into living a life in the Lord;
> Pressed into living a Christ-life outpoured.[87]

As with Jacob, when we wrestle with an issue and God does not prevail, He has to dislocate us. We are touched by God. Even the gentle touch of God on our lives seems to be a painful pressure. The carnal nature of our wrestling in the flesh is rendered powerless by a touch. We are weakened, weary from struggle, so we cannot rise without God's help

## Prevailing with God

In the end, if we are willing to wrestle, we will prevail, as did Jacob (v. 26-28). When we persevere through struggle—when we don't give up or avoid what God is confronting us with, then we will press through to victory and blessing. We cling on to God. We hold on and hold fast.

When Jacob persevered through the struggle, God changed his name to Israel—one who is God's struggler (v. 28). His name was changed—from deceiver to God's fighter. He was given a change of character, reputation, with a new nature, a new relationship with God. He received a new purpose—a new calling. His life was rescued from the quagmire of repeated deception. He had a new life message.

As we have a face-to-face encounter with God, we are transformed. He marveled that his life was preserved (v. 30).

God left Jacob with a perpetual reminder of what God had done and where he had come from (v. 31). God left him with a limp. God continually reminds us that it is His strength in the midst of our weakness. The mark of a man touched by God is humility (33:3).

At this point, the conflict is resolved (33:10). Our past has been dealt with. We see our enemy, our conflict, those whom we have wronged, as the face of God. He redeems our past so that He can guide us into our future.

## Forgetting Our Past

Someone has quipped, "If you are living in the past, you are history." Paul exhorted, "Forgetting what lies behind and reaching forward to what lies ahead, I press on toward the goal for the prize of the upward call of God in Christ Jesus" (Philippians 3:13-14, NASB). In order to achieve the goals and purposes God has for our lives, we need to leave the past behind. To forget the past does not mean to erase it from our memory. Rather, the Greek word for "forget" means to neglect or no longer care for. In other words, our past no longer matters. Our attitude toward the past is one of benign neglect. We no longer care about it. It no longer affects us in a negative way; it no longer causes us pain. Our focus is not on the past, but looking to Jesus and His future for our lives. We "forget those things that are behind," not by obliterating them from our memory, but by God's healing touch and a new, positive outlook on our negative experiences.

If we do not deal with past issues in our lives we will not find our niche. Issues such as unforgiveness, need to make restitution, character flaws, unresolved issues, people conflicts all need to be rectified before we can move on with God. Then we will no longer paralyzed by our past, and God's doors for our lives can be opened.

## GET BACK ON TRACK WHEN YOU THINK YOU'VE MISSED IT

I once saw an artist painting a beautiful picture of a nature scene. Then he took his paint brush, dipped it in black paint, and swept an ugly black streak across the canvas. The beautiful scene appeared to be ruined. But then he painted all around the streak, in the end making an even more beautiful painting than it was before. That is what God does with the ugly black marks of our lives.

To use another analogy, God is the great chess master. He knows our every move in advance, and is able to counter it and turn it around for good if we acknowledge our mistakes, repent of our self-efforts, and let Him take control once again. God takes our *mis*steps and makes them *His* steps.

Many years ago I made a big mistake in taking a position as a Christian school administrator and Assistant Pastor of Education in a certain church. There were indicators that I should not take the position, but I did not recognize them. The senior pastor of the church where I had been serving had met the pastor of the church where I was going to interview, and as a result told me, "I don't think you want to go there." When I went to interview for the position, one of the teachers of the Christian school pulled me aside and said, "You won't like it here." He didn't explain, but I thought he just meant the climate. I didn't catch his drift. My wife had hesitations, which I should have taken more seriously, but she was willing to go. I was between a rock and a hard place, especially financially, and I saw an open door, but not the cautions. I had resigned my former position, so had burnt my bridges behind me. I just assumed it was the will of the Lord.

Within a month of beginning the new position I knew I had made a mistake, but it took three months for me to admit it to my wife. I found out that the senior pastor of this church was a hyper-perfectionistic spiritual abuser, heaping unrealistic expectations, criticism, and guilt upon the church and school staff. I discovered that the entire situation was severely dysfunctional and that four of my staff were actually going through deep emotional problems or nervous breakdowns as a result of the pressure. One so badly affected her students by her emotional instability that I had to terminate her within three weeks of my arrival. Within six months, I was also nearly a casualty of a nervous breakdown. I had become a lightning rod of protection for my staff, deflecting the criticism away from them to myself. After several confrontations with the pastor (and not always handling it well), it was mutually agreed that we could not work together and the board gave me a generous severance package. It was a nightmare of a year, but God brought us through and I survived without any permanent scars.

Although my wife and I believed I had missed God's will, some of the church members and school staff felt that we were a godsend to bring hope and change and mediation to an unbearable situation. Students and staff had tears in their eyes and words of heartfelt appreciation at our farewell for the compassionate pastoral care I had given. So my missteps actually became His steps for ministering to hurting people.

I wish I could say that was the only big mistake I have made, but I could recite an entire litany of blunders. In each case, God has turned it around for good, overcoming my faults and making something beautiful out of an ugly circumstance.

When I was a child, we had a plastic, blow up, almost life-size cartoon character that was weighted down at the bottom. I would hit it again and again, and it would keep bouncing back up again. God intends for us to be like that bounce-back man. No matter how many times we are hit by the trials of life and our mistakes, we can be the "come-back kid." Proverbs 24:16 tells us, "For though a righteous man falls seven times, he rises again." This Scripture tells us, first of all, that the righteous do fall. Secondly, seven being the number of completion or perfection, the implication of this Scripture is that even though we fall seemingly totally and completely, we can get up again. Through Christ, we have a resiliency, an ability to bounce back from anything. Paul encourages us in 2 Corinthians 4:8-9 that even when it seems like we've gone down for the count, we may be "knocked down, but not knocked out" (J. B. Phillips paraphrase). God wants to turn our setbacks into comebacks.

How do we rise again after we have fallen? Here are eleven keys I have learned from my own experiences.

### Face Reality and Acknowledge Your Misstep.

First of all, we need to face reality and admit that we have missed it. We have a natural tendency to ignore or deny the handwriting on the wall. Confess it to the Lord and accept His forgiveness. Own up to it to whoever was affected by our mistake. It is hard for a man to admit to his wife that he has blown it, but eventually I had to "fess up." However, it took me three months to do so. I needed to swallow my pride.

### Accept the Consequences.

Even though we have been forgiven by the Lord, we still have to live with the results of our mistakes. God will eventually make something good out of it, but in the meantime, we will need to persevere through the natural costs of the blunder. For instance, a teenage girl who becomes pregnant has to face the consequences of her mistake—the shame and embarrassment—but a beautiful child is born.

Once I realized I had made a mistake accepting that position, I could not just get up and leave, so I endeavored to make the best of a bad situation. In the short term, it was miserable, but God worked good out of it in the long run.

### Overcome Condemnation.

While we still have to live with our mistakes, we must not let the forces of Satan condemn us and cause us to wallow in guilt, depression, and self-pity, or self-flagellation. I went over and over again the mire in which I had stepped. Finally, I just had to repeat over and over again the Scripture, "There is now no condemnation to those who are in Christ Jesus" (Romans 8:1). Conviction is from the Lord, but condemnation is from the devil. He is the "accuser of the brethren" (Revelation 12:10).

Revelation 12:11 gives us three keys to overcoming the accusations of Satan: "And they overcame him by the blood of the Lamb, the word of their testimony, and they loved not their souls unto death. Once we are forgiven, our sins are "under the blood," covered by the atoning sacrifice of Jesus Christ for our sins. We give positive testimony of what Christ has done in us—how He has forgiven us, changed us, and set us free, and give faith confessions of the truths of His Word. And we "love not our souls unto death." That means that we die to ourselves, our desires, our efforts, our attempts to save face.

Sometimes, when we are in the dumps, we have to resort to self-talk, like David did in Psalm 42:5, "Why are you downcast, O my soul? Why are so disturbed within me? Put your hope in God, for I will yet praise him, my Savior and my God." We can declare with Micah 7:8, "Though I have fallen, I will rise."

### Take God's Hand.

He will help us get back on our feet. We need to be in a place of total dependency upon Him. Sometimes, we have fallen because we made our own decision or action without hearing His counsel. Our mistakes make it all the more clear to us that it has to be God and His leading and His working, or we are nothing without Him. As Proverbs 3:5-6 counsels us, "Trust in the Lord with all your heart, and do not lean on your own understanding. In all your ways acknowledge Him, and He will make your paths straight" (NASB).

### Take Courage and Stand Again.

Some people are afraid or ashamed to get back up after they have fallen. Joshua was told time and again, "Take courage. . . . Take courage. . . . Take courage." We get back up, dust our selves off, and resume living our lives, this time with God's help. We get back on course through prayer, trust, and obedience.

### Learn from Your Mistake.

Consider what insights you can glean for the future so that you don't make the same mistake again. What would you differently? How can you avoid this kind of problem in the future, or handle it better? Consider also what life message God would have you share with others regarding this mistake. As noted earlier, Bill Gothard tells us that our message is forged out of our failures. You can learn to listen more closely to the voice of God, His urgings and cautions.

### See Your Fall from God's Perspective.

God is not going to condemn us for falling. He knows we are but little children learning to walk, so bids us as a loving Father to get up and walk again. He is watching over us, and will make something good out of a bad situation. God's grace is greater than our biggest mistakes. He is able to redeem our failures. Remember that we are saints in process. God is not finished with us yet. My Scottish-Irish Grandmother King used to say, "Children and fools should not look at half-done work." I remember in a meeting years ago seeing Corrie Ten Boom holding up the back of a tapestry, saying that we only see the backside with all its snarls, tangles, shapelessness, and disharmony. But God looks at the front of the tapestry to the elegant finished product. Paul reminds us, "He who began a good work in you will perfect it until the day of Christ Jesus" (Philippians 1:6, NASB).

### Give a Sacrifice of Praise.

Look back at the times of trouble and adversity and be able to praise God without cynicism. In the words of a popular chorus, "Give thanks with a grateful heart . . . ." Habakkuk 3:17-19 exhorts us:

> Though the fig tree does not bud and there are no grapes on
>     the vines,
> though the olive crop fails and the fields produce no food,
> though there are no sheep in the pen and no cattle in the stalls,
> yet I will rejoice in the Lord,
> I will be joyful in God my Savior.
> The Sovereign Lord is my strength;
> he makes my feet like the feet of a deer,
> he enables me to go on the heights.

Even in our times of failure and missteps, we can be grateful that God is bringing us through. Our attitude in these times will determine our altitude. If we maintain a right spirit and praise God, we will rise once more.

## Seek God More Intensely.

Experiences like these can lead us to seek the presence of God in greater ways than we have before. Mistakes can actually push us into His presence. Then we can learn to delight in Him all the more.

## Ask God to Intervene.

Realize that only God can reverse the curse in your life. John Bradley observes, "As I have witnessed too many down-spiraling lives, I have found that only something supernatural can break the deadlock. It starts with a willingness to seek help."[88] Be willing to pray, "Have mercy on me, O God."

## Get Back on Course.

You may have taken a detour from God's desire for your life, but He has been with you on that detour and will guide you back to the right path. It may take longer than God originally intended, but He will use a different route, take you on a different course to accomplish His will. He *can* cause all things to work together for good (Romans 8:28).

Listen for the voice of God, and wait on Him to answer, rather than striking out on your own self-efforts and inclinations. Do what you know He wants you to do—"trust and obey, for there's no other way to be happy in Jesus, but to trust and obey."

## FORGIVE AND BE FORGIVEN

One of the biggest stumbling blocks that prevent people from moving on to find their niche in God's plan is unforgiveness. Either we have not dealt with sin in our own life and asked the forgiveness of others, or we do not forgive others their sins against us.

Jesus made it clear that our regular practice of prayer needs to be "Forgive us our trespasses as we forgive those who trespass against us."

## Search Your Heart and Ask for Forgiveness

As a young adult, I was involved in youth ministry on the staff of Young Life as well as a church youth pastor. I attended Bill Gothard's "Seminar in Basic Youth Conflicts," thinking I would gain insights for counseling teenagers. However, God was working in my life to deal with unresolved conflicts with my parents from my teen years. As Gothard dealt with the need clearing our slate of unresolved issues from our own past, I became aware that in order for me to be effective in ministering to teens I needed to ask my parents for forgiveness for my attitudes, even as a Christian teenager. It took me about three months to get up the courage to do it, but it brought great healing and reconciliation between me and my parents. It also opened the floodgates for greater ministry to teens and their relationships with their parents.

If there is anyone whom you have offended, before you can move forward with your life, before you can find your niche, you will need to make amends. Seek to be reconciled. Before Jacob could move into God's Promised Land for his life, he had to make amends with his brother. Pray the words of David, "Search me, O God, and know my heart; test me and know my anxious thoughts. See if there is any offensive way in me, and lead me in the way everlasting" (Psalm 139:23-24).

## Forgive and Forbear Others

If you are going to be involved in service for God, forgiving others is absolutely essential. You will be lied to, lied about, slandered, manipulated, taken advantage of, deceived, yelled at, threatened, and more— even by other Christians. If you are to survive and move ahead with your life, you must forgive. The Apostle re-emphasized the teaching of Jesus, exhorting, "Bear with one another and forgive whatever grievances you may have against one another. Forgive as the Lord forgave you" (Colossians 3:13).

Have you discovered that some of your deepest offenses and hurts come from fellow Christians? We say, "Well I could take that from an unbeliever, but he's a Christian, he should know better." Why is it we are offended so often by our brothers and sisters in Christ? Two main reasons: First, we are "saints in process" – we are not perfect. The closer to each then we become in Christ, the more we grate on each other, the more we reveal one another's weaknesses as well as our deepest hurts from our most intimate friends – because we put them on a pedestal. Secondly, because we are in process, God wants to use our rubbing shoulders with one another to expose and bring to the surface hidden within our lives – so He can deal with them openly

Since we will tend to offend each other more as part of God's purpose, He has provided the healing salve for those hurts and wounds in the Body of Christ—patience, forgiveness, forbearance and love. They all work together to bring healing to the Body. Someone has said that forgiveness is the great difference between Christianity and all other religions. So the main key to effective witness and ministry is to show the healing power of forgiveness to bring restoration and reconciliation.

In a church where I pastored, the wife of one of the deacons became so upset with me that she would not talk to me. She would slam a door in my face. Before an annual church business meeting the Lord revealed to me supernaturally that I would be verbally attacked in that meeting, but took me to 1 Peter 2:24 to follow the example of Jesus, who spoke not a word when He was reproached. Sure enough, this woman got up in the meeting and raked me over the coals about how poor a pastor I was. And as my face flushed red, God told me to be silent. Some of my closest supporters asked me later why I didn't put her in her place. I told them what the Lord had told me, and they just shook their heads.

I continued to show love and friendliness to this woman over the next three months in spite of the cold shoulder she continued to give me. She eventually came to me and my wife for counseling. One Sunday morning soon after counseling with her she stood up in a Sunday morning worship service. I thought, "Oh no, here it comes again." Instead, she repented in front of the whole congregation, saying that she had put me through hell. She became one of my ardent supporters—all because I was willing to forgive her.

What happens when we remain bitter, resentful, or intolerant, failing to forgive? If we continue to hold a grudge or a chip on our shoulder, layers of bitterness build up and our heats become hardened. Unforgiveness can cause many negative effects on our lives:

- *It affects our health.* Colitis, fatigue, loss of sleep, depression, goiter, high blood pressure, ulcers, arthritis, headaches, and bone disease can all be caused by bitterness due to becoming emotionally upset, tense, or irritable. Medical doctor S. I. McMillen, in his book *None of These Diseases*, affirms, "It's not what you eat, but what eats you."[89]
- *It affects our relationships with our family, church, and others.* The author of Hebrews warns, "See that no one comes short of the grace of God, that not root of bitterness springing up causes trouble, and by it many be defiled." (Hebrews 12:15, NASB). Love and bitterness cannot co-exist, so it will cause poisoning of family and interpersonal relationships, and result in more irritation, discord, disharmony and disunity. The entire community of faith can become defiled.

- *It affects our prayer life and fellowship with God.* "If you do not forgive others, your Father will not forgive your transgressions" (Matthew 6:15, NASB).
- *It affects our freedom.* You become in bondage to the one you won't forgive, and may even become like that person because of an emotional focus. You can become a prisoner of resentment.
- *It affects our ability to overcome Satan and gain victory.* You grieve the Holy Spirit and give the devil a foothold (Ephesians 4:27, 30).
- *It affects our service for God.* Your ministry is made ineffective. You become a poor witness and insensitive to needs. Dwight Moody declared that an unforgiving spirit quenches revival and blocks the power of the Holy Spirit. "They will know you are Christians by your love," the 1970s song proclaims. Where there is no forgiveness, there is no love, and thus no ministry. Proverbs 6:19 says that God detests those who "stir up dissension among brothers." Disharmony among Christians will quench love, peace, and unity and will block effective witness and ministry.

If you will confess sin of unforgiveness and release the healing power of forgiveness, it will open doors for ministry, bring peace and reconciliation and harmony, trigger answers to prayer, and stir opportunities for sharing your faith. Dallas Willard writes with insight, "Forgiving is but one case of giving, and one who does not forgive does not live in the spiritual atmosphere and reality of giving, where prayers are answered."[90] No matter what anyone has done to you, in order to move on with God, you need to forgive that person. If we do not forgive, we cannot expect to find God's niche for our lives.

## ABANDON MEDIOCRITY AND PURSUE EXCELLENCE

As I mentioned in an earlier chapter, Oswald Chambers has said that good can be the enemy of the best. Sometimes our own mediocrity or half-heartedness, being content with just getting by rather than pursuing after excellence in our lives and work, can prevent God's best from opening up for us. Diligence is key in moving ahead with God's purposes for our life:

"The plans of the diligent lead to profit" (Proverbs 21:5).
"Diligent hands will rule" (Proverbs 12:24).
"The desires of the diligent are fully satisfied" (Proverbs 13:4).

"Be diligent in these matters; give yourself wholly to them, so that everyone may see your progress" (1 Timothy 4:15).

Paul himself modeled the pursuit of excellence: "I press on toward the goal to win the prize for which God has called me heavenward in Christ Jesus" (Philippians 3:14).

Our motivation for excellence is not ultimately for our own personal benefit, but for the glory of God, because we have been called by His glory and excellence (1 Peter 1:3). "Do your best to present yourself to God as one approved, a workman who does not need to be ashamed" (2 Timothy 2:15). "Whatever you do, work at it with all your heart, as working for the Lord, not for men" (Colossians 3:23).

Doing our very best for the glory of God will open up new doors for God to fulfill His purposes through our lives. Solomon assured, "Do you see a man skilled in his work? He will serve before kings; he will not serve before obscure men" (Proverbs 22:29). Isaiah recognized this principle, writing, "A noble man makes noble plans and by noble plans he stands." (Isaiah 32:8, NASB). The Hebrew word for "noble" here means to impel oneself. Charles Paul Conn writes of the importance of impelling our selves nobly toward excellence:

Whatever it is,
however impossible it seems,
whatever the obstacle that lies between you and it,
if it is noble,
if it is consistent with God's kingdom,
you must hunger after it and stretch yourself to reach it.[91]

Faithfulness in the little things produces excellence, which opens greater doors for our lives. As Jesus said, "He who is faithful in little will be faithful in much." Solomon wrote that "the little foxes spoil the vines" (Song of Solomon 2:15, KJV). Just think if your surgeon did not pursue excellence. A quarter of an inch in an incision can sometimes mean the difference in life or death. The one thing you don't want to hear a surgeon say is "Oops!"

One of the things that I learned in doing doctoral work, is that excellence means making sure that the details are correct—grammar, spelling, exactness and consistency in form and style, even in every detail of footnoting and bibliographic format. I had to go over things again . . . and again . . . and again . . . to get them right. In the early chapters of my doctoral dissertation, I had to submit chapter revisions as many as six times. But that is the price to pay in becoming a "doctor."

Paul prays that "you may approve the things that are excellent" (Philippians 1:10, NASB), and exhorts us to let our minds dwell on things that are excellent (Philippians 4:8). He praised the Thessalonians that they excelled, but encouraged them to "excel still more" (NASB) in several areas of their lives:

- Their walk or conduct – 4:1
- Pleasing God – 4:1
- Loving one another – 4:10
- Enlarging their faith – 1:3

Peter likewise exhorts to increasing in godly qualities (2 Peter 1:3-8), affirming, "For if these qualities are yours and are increasing, they render you neither useless nor unfruitful in the true knowledge of our Lord Jesus Christ" (2 Peter 1:8, NASB).

We may think we are doing well, but we always need to be teachable and willing to grow, willing to excel even more. Even though I have public speaking skills, I am always seeking to learn how I can communicate more effectively through preaching and teaching. Paul, probably the greatest Christian who ever lived, admitted of himself, "Not that I have obtained all this, or have already been made perfect, but I press on to take hold of that for which Christ Jesus took hold of me" (Philippians 3:12). Ask others what areas they think you can seek to excel more in your life.

## FOR FURTHER REFLECTION

1. What are your current ambitions and plans? Have you surrendered them to the Lord?

2. Is there anything between you and God? What is God dealing with in your life? What is your river Jabbok, or your Esau?

3. Where is God applying pressure? What is He putting His finger on? What is He shaking? What is the point of conflict? Are you willing to change and be changed?

4. What things from your past do you need to no longer care about? How can you act with benign neglect about those things from the past?

5. Describe a time you believe you missed God's will. What lesson did you learn from the mistake?

6. How can God make something good out of your mistake? Can you trust Him to do so?

7. How can you get back on course to accomplish God's will in your life?

8. Who do you need to forgive? To whom do you need to ask forgiveness?

9. What is mediocre in your life that you can improve upon? In what areas of your life can you pursue excellence?

# Manage Yourself

*"If anyone does not know how to manage his family, how can he take care of God's church?"* (1 Timothy 3:4).

In order to find our niche, we need to be good managers or stewards of what God has given us charge over. As mentioned in Chapter 4, a steward is a servant in charge. Paul instructed Timothy that a church leader must manage his household well (1 Timothy 3:4, 12). So it is in every calling, we must be effective, responsible managers of our "household"—that is, of ourselves and all that God has entrusted under our care. The principle is if we can't handle something smaller, we cannot handle something larger. So we have to be able to manage ourselves in order to find our niche and go on to greater things in God. When we manage ourselves, then we can open the doors for promotion, to be given greater authority and responsibility as a servant in charge.

God has given us at least nine areas to demonstrate wise, faithful stewardship: disciplined living, time and priorities, abilities, finances, attitudes, thought life, relationship conflicts, tongue and anger, and appetites.

## MANAGE YOURSELF THROUGH SELF-DISCIPLINE

We manage ourselves and all that God has entrusted us through self-discipline. Paul counseled Timothy, "Discipline yourself for the purpose of godliness" (1 Timothy 4:7). Self-discipline is an essential character quality. It is a fruit of the Spirit. Not everyone who is self-disciplined is mature, but you cannot become mature without a good measure of self-discipline. John Maxwell, in his highly-acclaimed book *Developing the Leader Within You*, writes that self-discipline is the "price tag to leadership." He explains that the Greek word for self-control "describes people who are willing to get a grip on their lives and take control of areas that will bring them success or failure."[92]

If we do not discipline ourselves, we will be disciplined by the Lord through circumstances and others. The Holy Spirit within us desires to bear the fruit of self-discipline within our lives, but we must cooperate with the Holy Spirit in order for Him to be able to work. How do we become self-disciplined?

First of all, we deny ourselves. We need to be willing to hold back our own personal desires. Second, Paul exhorts, "Endure hardship as a good soldier of Christ." (2 Timothy 2:3). He gives the image of a soldier, a runner, and a farmer, all who make a disciplined extra effort and endure through hardship.

## MANAGE YOUR TIME AND PRIORITIES

In order to find our niche, we need to reorder our life. As we seek first God's kingdom and righteousness, all that we need will be supplied to us (Matthew 6:33). Paul counsels, "Redeem (make the most of) the time, for the days are evil." (Ephesians 5:17). Many times failure to find our niche may be due to missed opportunities, in which we have failed to make the best use of our time.

I remember many years ago one of my professors saying, "If you want to be a biblical scholar, you will need to give up the comic strips." Now, I must admit that I never completely gave up the comic page. However, I did discover while working intensively on my doctoral dissertation that scholarship means giving up trivial pursuits and rearranging priorities. I no longer had time to linger long over the comic page or sports page or work on crossword puzzles. Not that there is anything wrong with them, but the focus of my attention had changed. And that does not mean that I did not have leisure time, but the types of leisurely activities I engage in have changed since then.

Solomon in his wisdom counseled that there is a time and a procedure for everything (Ecclesiastes 3:1; 8:6). Much of our ineffectiveness is due to lack of organization, failure to establish an orderly, disciplined, timely process.

## MANAGE YOUR ABILITIES

Peter exhorted, "As each one has received a special gift, employ it in serving one another, as good stewards of the manifold grace of God" (1 Peter 4:10). For many years I was caught up in the busyness of pastoral ministry and neglected the gift of writing God had given to me. My District Superintendent encouraged me to stir up the gift within, so I began writing again. The first few things I wrote were rejected, so I was tempted to give up. But an urging within stirred me to write, so I persevered until an article was accepted. Then it opened the door to other writing opportunities. If you will make use of the abilities you have, even if seemingly unsuccessful initially, God will enhance your abilities and open locked doors.

There is always room for improvement and further development of the abilities God has given us. Paul counseled Timothy, "Kindle afresh the gift of God which is in you" (2 Tim. 1:6). We need to stir up the abilities God has given us and let Him show us how to enhance His working through us.

## MANAGE YOUR FINANCES

Someone has said, "Money management is self-management." Someone else has quipped, "Money is a good servant, but a poor master." Perhaps no other area of our life demonstrates our ability to manage ourselves as how we manage our finances. Jesus declared that he who is faithful in little will be faithful in much and he who is unfaithful in little will be unfaithful in much (Luke 16:10-12). Accomplishing God's full purposes for our lives involves wise stewardship of the money with which God has entrusted us. Unbridled or impulsive spending costs us squandered opportunities to fulfill God's will.

*Tithe your income.* Some will argue that tithing is under the Law of the Old Covenant and not for today. In reality, the New Testament principle is giving 100%, not merely 10%. Tithing is only the starting point of generosity. Oral Roberts encourages people to view tithing not as a debt you owe, but as a seed you sow. Paul avowed, "If you sow sparingly, you will reap sparingly." You will never fulfill God's purposes for your life until you know the joy of being a cheerful (Greek, *hilarion*) giver, giving "hilariously" (2 Corinthians 9:6)

I know from more than forty years of experience the value of tithing. Ever since my paper route as a twelve-year old boy, I have tithed my income, and seen God bless abundantly. Even during times when I was virtually unemployed, I tithed what little income I received, and God always made a way.

When I became engaged to my wife Kathy, I urged us together to tithe our income. She balked at the idea at first because the church she grew up in never stressed tithing. She did not see the value in it, and it seemed to her extreme. How would we ever live on so much less? A few weeks after our wedding, the church where I was serving as assistant pastor gave us a "preacher pounding." That does not mean that the church beat up on us. Rather, they gave "a pound of this and a pound of that"—in foods, dry goods, and supplies.

God promises that when we tithe He will pour out a blessing from heaven so great that there will not be enough room to contain it (Malachi 3:10). This literally happened to us. We received so much from the "preacher pounding" that there was not enough room in our little one-bedroom duplex to contain all that had been given! Kathy saw first hand the promise of Malachi 3:10 fulfilled.

*Get out and stay out of debt.* When we first got married we had several thousand dollars in educational and auto loans. In our first year of marriage Kathy and I committed to getting out of debt and staying out of debt—never taking out a loan for anything depreciating in value. So for the first year and a half of marriage, we lived off my salary (about $6000 a year in the mid-1970s), and committed her salary as a teacher (which was much more than my salary) toward paying off our loans. And in less than two years the loans were completely paid off.

Ever since that time we have never taken out a car loan and have only paid $25 in credit card debt in more than 30 years of marriage (we do have a mortgage on our house, but the home and property appreciate in value). Instead of paying $200 a month for a car loan, we put $200 a month in a savings account for a car. We pay off our credit card charges every month and don't charge anything we cannot pay within 30 days. Now we haven't always new cars or had the first and best of everything, but God has always provided for our needs. We took out a few thousand dollars in educational loans for our son in college (no interest charges until after graduation), but set aside money in an educational account and paid the loans off in full before the interest charges began to kick in.

I share this not to brag, but to show that it can be done. It means sometimes denying yourself, but God rewards self-denial with greater blessings and provisions. So I encourage you to find your niche by managing your finances and becoming debt free.

*Live simply, spend wisely, and handle prosperity with discernment.* Richard Foster writes of what he calls the "discipline of simplicity," saying, "Simplicity is freedom. . . . Simplicity brings joy and balance."[93] Among the principles of simplicity he includes the following:

- Buy things for their usefulness rather than their status.
- Reject anything that is producing an addiction in you.

- Develop a habit of giving things away. . . . De-accumulate!
- Refuse to be propagandized by the custodians of modern gadgetry.
- Learn to enjoy things without owning them.
- Develop a deeper appreciation for the creation.
- Look with healthy skepticism at all "buy now, pay later" schemes.
- Obey Jesus' instructions about plain, honest speech.
- Reject anything that breeds the oppression of others.
- Shun anything that distracts you from seeking first the kingdom of God.[94]

When God prospers us, we need to be able to enjoy what God has provided without self-indulgence. A. B. Simpson spoke of the "discipline of prosperity":

How few Christians really know how to abound. How frequently prosperity changes their temper and the habits and fruits of their lives! To receive God's blessing in temporal things, to have wealth suddenly thrust upon us, to be surrounded with the congenial friends, to be enriched with all the happiness that love, home the world's applause and unbounded prosperity can give, and yet to keep a humble heart, to be separated from the world in its spirit and in its pleasures, to keep our hearts in holy indifference from the love and need of earthly things, . . . and to use our prosperity and wealth as a sacred trust for Him, counting nothing our own, and still depending upon Him as simply as in the days of penury—this, indeed, is an experience rarely found, and only possible through the infinite grace of God.[95]

Prosperity may break or ruin a person who does not know how to handle it, or who does not have his or her character developed sufficiently.

## MANAGE YOUR ATTITUDES

Your *attitude* determines your *altitude*. Paul's letter to the Philippians is filled with exhortations about attitude. Paul admonished, "Do all things without grumbling and disputing" (Philippians 2:14). On the positive side, he exhorted, "Finally, Brethren, whatever is true, whatever is honorable, whatever is right, whatever is pure, whatever is lovely, whatever is of good repute, if there is any excellence and if anything worthy of praise, let your mind dwell on these things" (Philippians 4:8). He repeatedly commanded the Philippians to rejoice (Philippians 4:4).

I remember a clip from an old Bob Newburn show in which as a psychologist he was counseling a person, saying, "Stop it! Just stop it!" Paul approached Christians in his letters in a similar manner. He commanded people, "Stop your behavior" or "Just do it." Our attitudes are a matter of choice. We may be in an unpleasant or desperate situation, but we can choose how we will respond—in anger, fear, anxiety, and despair—or in peace, joy, love, self-control, etc. What we speak with our lips and on what our minds dwell affects our attitudes and our ability to rise above difficult situations.

John Maxwell writes that leaders' "dispositions are more important than their positions."[96] Some attitudes that hinder finding our niche include the following:

*Unteachableness.* I once hired a principal for our Christian school who was capable but unteachable. He believed he knew it all and did not need to be taught. When he and the school staff attended a conference, rather than attending seminar sessions with his staff, he went out to play golf. Needless to say, he did not last long at our school.

Another young man I was mentoring for the ministry became independent in spirit and not willing to take counsel. When he was interviewed for licensing, his attitude of unteachableness was evident to the Licensing Council. As a result, he was not accepted for licensing, and because of his subsequent bitterness and pride, he even dropped out of church for a time. If we are not teachable, we are not worthy of leading or teaching others.

*Ingratitude.* When I was selling jewelry years ago while pastoring a small congregation, I complained to one of my mentors about how I disliked the job and felt like I needed to be in full-time ministry in another church setting. He firmly, but gently, rebuked me for looking down on the job. I didn't take his rebuke to heart at the time, feeling he just didn't understand what I was going through. But before the Lord could open up full-time ministry to me, I had to learn to be grateful for the job He had provided and content to remain in the position until He saw fit to release me. I wasn't in my niche, but God had some work to do in me before I was ready for His ultimate role for me.

*A critical spirit.* If we are constantly critical of others and engage in fault-finding, it will affect our ability to find our niche. Earlier in my ministry, I was ruled by my perfectionism. Not only would be hard on myself, but I would be hard on others. My performance orientation actually kept me from performing well. I lost influence because of my critical spirit and demands upon others.

## MANAGE YOUR THOUGHT LIFE

Related to our attitudes is our thought life—what we think about throughout the day, on what our mind dwells. Our problems belong with our thoughts. As we mentioned in Key #1, Proverbs 23:7 tells us, "As a man thinks in his heart, so is he." We are what we think. Our thought life must be self-disciplined or we may not find our niche. If we just let our thoughts go, they will follow the second law of thermodynamics—the law of entropy—that if left to ourselves our minds will spiral downward. That is why Paul exhorts us to cast down imaginations, break down strongholds, and "bring every thought captive to the obedience of Christ." If we do not control our thoughts, our thoughts will control us. If we do not actively reject and resist thoughts of fear, depression, condemnation, anger, lust, doubt, suspicion, etc., when they come into our mind, they will play games with our mind. We will be pulled down by such thoughts. They will keep us from the diligence and excellence that open doors for us to find our niche.

Wrong thoughts lead to wrong imaginations; wrong imaginations lead to wrong actions; wrong actions repeated and not repented of lead to bad habits; bad habits lead to loss of sensitivity to the Holy Spirit and His promptings, which in turn leads to deception and influence from unholy spirits. Deception and unholy supernatural influences (evil spirits) result in bondage.

The converse is also true: Right thoughts lead to sanctified imagination (seeing with the eyes of faith), which then leads to right actions. Right actions repeated form godly habits, and result in greater sensitivity to the Holy Spirit. The Holy Spirit leads us into all truth, and the truth sets us free (John 8:32). We become free to be and do all that God desires, to find our niche. Freedom in Christ opens doors that had been bound shut.

Paul exhorts us, "Finally, brothers, whatever is true, whatever is noble, whatever is right, whatever is pure, whatever is lovely, whatever is admirable—if anything is excellent or praiseworthy—think about such things." (Philippians 4:8). These will bring about success in your endeavors for the kingdom of God.

## MANAGE YOUR RELATIONSHIP CONFLICTS

*"If it is possible, as far as it depends on you, live at peace with everyone"* (Romans 12:8).

Finding our purpose involves relationships with people. Conflicts are inevitable in relationships. An old poem says it well:

"O, to dwell above with saints we love—that will be glory! To dwell below with saints we know—now that's another story!

One of the keys to success is learning to manage conflict. We want to be overcomers, but without overcoming anything. Someone has said, "Problem-solving is the gateway to leadership." If we manage our conflicts and solve problems, we will find that our niche will open up to us. Until we learn to manage our relationships—people who demonstrate co-dependency, controlling people, unreasonable, compulsive, impulsive, passive, aggressive, etc. we will not be able to move into God's full purposes for our lives.

I floundered in the relationships in my ministry until I read a book and attended a seminar on coping with difficult people.[97] One problem I discovered was that having grown up in Pennsylvania, we Northeasterners tend to be straight forward, speaking forthrightly what we think. But living in Oklahoma I was perceived as being blunt and rude. I was puzzled by why people were offended by my words. I would think, "What did I say that was so bad?" Then I realized that the Oklahoma way is to talk around the subject, not to come right out and say what is on your mind. Thus I had many conflicts with people until I learned how to blend with Southern culture and watch my words and tones carefully. (It helped that I married a native Okie!) If we have not learned the social skills of handling the attitudes, behaviors, and reactions of others, it can prevent us from becoming all that God wants us to be. If you have a need in this area, you might want to take a seminar in dealing with difficult people, like the one I took through Career Track.

## MANAGE YOUR TONGUE AND YOUR ANGER

*"Consider what a great forest is set on fire by a small spark. The tongue also is a fire, a world of evil among the parts of the body. It corrupts the whole person, sets the whole course of his life on fire, and is itself set on fire by hell"* (James 3:5-6).

*"In your anger do not sin, , , , Do not give the devil a foothold. . . . do not let any unwholesome talk come out of your mouths, but only what is helpful for others according to their needs, that it may benefit those who listen"* (Ephesians 4:26, 27, 29).

Related to managing conflict is managing our tongue, because our words are often the source of our conflict. Once while I was getting a haircut at a Christian-owned hair salon, the woman who was cutting my hair told me she believed God had a calling on her life, but she realized that her mouth kept her from moving into her ministry. She was wise enough to realize that she could not find her niche until she made an effort to control her tongue.

When I was young, I had a sharp tongue and a short fuse. While I was a freshman in college, I got into a theological debate with my roommate, a PK (Preacher's Kid). I spoke some strong, cutting words about how his behavior did not square with his theology. In very unflattering terms, I implied he was a hypocrite. I thought I was speaking the truth, but it sure wasn't in love. He did not take it well, and we both became so angry, we ended up in a fist fight. Here he a PK, and I, a pre-ministerial student, were coming to blows over biblical interpretation! And I had to eat my own words about practicing what I preach.

It still took several years to sanctify my Irish red-haired temper. As a young pastor, when I was criticized, I could retaliate eloquently and incisively. Funny though, others didn't think it was so eloquent. My angry reactions got me into many church-related conflicts, as well as losing respect with some church members and leaders. Fortunately, the Lord has quieted my sharp tongue and wit (on most occasions) and taught me the value of being "quick to listen, slow to speak and slow to become angry" (James 1:19). Now, friends and co-workers find it hard to believe that I had such a caustic tongue. The Lord has worked in me a gentleness and patience that has enabled me to build fruitful relationships with others and minister broadly and ecumenically in many denominations and theological persuasions. I was even asked to serve on a commission that dialogues about various theological disagreements.

If you will manage your words and your temper, God will open doors to place you in strategic opportunities to diffuse toxic conversation and foster reconciliation.

## MANAGE YOUR APPETITES

*"Abstain from fleshly lusts which war against the soul"*
(1 Peter 2:11).

*"Let your moderation be known unto all men"*
(Philippians 4:5, KJV).

*"I buffet my body and make it my slave, lest possibly, after I have
preached to others, I myself should be disqualified."*
(1 Corinthians 9:27, NASB).

Managing our appetites means disciplining ourselves to deny certain comforts or pleasures for the purpose of maintaining healthy moderation or balance in our lives. Part of self-discipline is learning moderation in all things—what we eat, drink, indulge in. God wants us to enjoy life, but sometimes we cannot find our niche because we have not found a place of moderation, healthy balance in our life between what we enjoy and do.

The New American Standard Version of 1 Corinthians 9:24 uses the term "buffet" (meaning to be hard on oneself). However, some people act as if it means buffet yourself (at a food buffet), just the opposite of what God wants to accomplish. Paul admits that if he did not buffet himself, if he was not strict on his bodily appetites, he could be disqualified from ministry. Oftentimes, our human desires get in the way of God's assignment for our lives.

One way to manage your appetites is to practice fasting. There are many kinds of fasts. Historic churches have used the period of time before Easter known as Lent to practice self-denial of certain things for 40 days. Daniel speaks of a vegetable only diet at a certain period of time, and at another time, a fast of "no pleasant food" for three weeks. I know a woman who went on what she called a "praise fast" in which she fasted from chocolate for forty days along with a commitment not to grumble or complain, but to give thanks and praise to the Lord. On the very first day of her fast, all hell broke loose on her job and everything went wrong! What a challenge from the Enemy! But she overcame and got the victory.

When I went on a low carbohydrate diet to deal with high triglycerides (fat cells in the blood), I had to cut back on or give up many of my favorite high carb foods—rice, potatoes, pasta, and of course, sweets. I lost 25 pounds in three months and got my triglycerides and lipids to safe levels. This was a kind of fast to moderate my diet.

There are other appetites to manage as well. You may need to fast from talking, from spending money, from ways in which you use your time. All of these disciplines can be keys to opening the doors to God's niche for your life.

On the other hand, some people can be overly-disciplined, over-regulated, not allowing them space for enjoyment or spontaneity. Discipline can become an obsessive-compulsion for some. At one point in my life, I would buy a soda pop from a machine, rather than inside a convenience store in order to save the few pennies of sales tax. It would drive my wife crazy! Ecclesiastes 7:16 warns about being "over-righteous," meaning, overly religious, strict, or legalistic. There is a fine balance between healthy discipline and unhealthy asceticism. Obsessive discipline can block God's placement for our lives just as an undisciplined lifestyle.

## FOR FURTHER REFLECTION

1. In what ways do you need to become more self-disciplined?

2. In what ways can you become a more effective manager of the time God has given you?

3. What priorities do you need to rearrange in your life?

4. How can you become a better steward of the finances God has entrusted to you?

5. What attitudes do you need to change and how can you change them?

6. How do you cope with conflicts and difficult people in your life?

7. What appetites or desires do you need to bring under control in your life?

# Open the Door to Your Niche

*"There is a time for everything, and a season for every activity under heaven."* (Ecclesiastes 3:1).

*"See, I have placed before you an open door that no one can shut"* (Revelation 3:8).

There is a time to sow and a time to reap, a time to wait on the Lord and a time to launch out in obedience and faith. To be ready to open the door and launch out into God's assignment for your life, you can begin by considering the nature, value and significance of the call and destiny God has for your life. Second, be prepared to enlarge your tents—to broaden your vision. Third, be willing to take a risk and launch out into the deep. Finally, take the plunge and go do it!

## CONSIDER YOUR CALLING AND DESTINY

*"For consider your call, brethren, that there were not many wise according to the flesh, not many mighty, not many noble. . ."* (1 Corinthians 1:26, NASB).

Have you considered the significance of your calling? To whatever God has called you, He wants you to consider the nature, value and significance of your calling.

### *Your Calling Is a HIGH Calling.*

*"I press on toward mark of the prize of the **high** calling of God in Christ Jesus"* (Philippians 3:14, KJV).

Your call is ever upward. When you find your niche, you will be challenged to go higher, or as C. S. Lewis has written, "further up and further in." There is no plateau in the Christian life. If you plateau, you become stagnant.

## *Your Calling Is a HEAVENLY Calling*

*"Therefore, holy brothers, who share in the **heavenly** calling, fix your thoughts on Jesus, the apostle and high priest whom we confess"* (Hebrews 3:1)

Our calling is not merely a high calling, but the highest calling—a heavenly calling. In fact, Paul tells us, "And God raised us up with Christ in the heavenly realms" (Ephesians 2:6). Your niche is in the heavenly places. A. B. Simpson discovered that heavenly calling and wrote a song, "I have found a heaven below; I am living in the glory." I began to discover that heavenly calling when the Lord once exhorted me through a prophetic word:

I am calling my people higher. I am calling you to set your eyes on the heavens, not on the earth. I call you to walk by faith, not by sight. You have set your sights on earthly things. You have set your sights too low. You have settled for too little. Your vision has been too short-sighted. I would call you to a higher vision, a clearer vision. I would take the scales off your eyes, and let you see the unseen, the invisible, the heavenly.

You are held to the earth by the law of gravity, the law of the flesh that holds you down. You overcome the law of gravity by the law of thrust. The law of thrust is stepping out and walking by faith. Faith is the rocket booster to overcome the gravity of the flesh. Let your faith become airborne. Let not the Enemy make you think you cannot overcome the law of gravity of the flesh. Set your sights on the heavens. Expand your vision. When you open your eyes and have the scales lifted, faith will arise in you and you will be held down no longer. You will overcome.

## *Your Calling Is a HOLY Calling*

*"But join with me in suffering for the gospel, by the power of God, who saved us and called us to a **holy** life"* (2 Timothy 1:9)

Your calling sets you apart. That is holiness. You are set apart to God as His special treasured possession. Your calling will help others to see that they are God's treasured possession as well

Your calling sets you apart from sin and the world. Thus Paul exhorts, "I urge you to live a life worthy of the calling you have received" (Ephesians 4:1). Your calling will lead others to become set apart from all that separates people from God, from all that hinders intimate communion with God.

Holiness is cleansing, purifying. Your calling calls you to purity, to be cleansed of all that is unclean. Your calling will also bring cleansing and purifying to others.

Holiness is the impartation of the character of Jesus Christ within yourself—the fruit of the Spirit. Your calling will bid you to be like Jesus. Your calling will stir others to be like Jesus.

Holiness is wholeness. You calling will produce in you wholeness for your entire spirit and soul and body (1 Thessalonians 5:23). Your calling will bring wholeness to others.

## Your Calling Is a HOPEFUL Calling

*"I pray also that the eyes of your heart may be enlightened in order that you may know the hope to which he has called you"* (Ephesians 1:18).

God has called you to hope. The biblical concept of hope is not wishful thinking, but rather confident expectation. You may have had difficulty in finding your niche, but God wants to give you hope—anticipation that He is at work and has purpose for your life. The promise of God to Israel in the exile is applicable to your life as well: "'For I know the plans I have for you,' declares the Lord, 'plans to prosper your and not to harm you, plans to give you hope and a future'" (Jeremiah 29:11). God wants you to realize your destiny:

- *You are destined to be an adopted child of God*—Ephesians 1:5

- *You are destined for an inheritance from God*—Ephesians 1:11 "When Joshua was old and well advanced in years, the Lord said to him, 'You are very old, and there are still very large areas of land to be taken over" (Joshua 13:1).

- *You are destined to be to the praise of God's glory.* In fact, three times in Ephesians, Paul emphasizes that we are destined to the praise of God's glory:

"He predestined us to be adopted as his sons through Jesus Christ, in accordance with his pleasure and will—*to the praise of his glorious grace*" (v. 5-6)

"In him we were also chosen, having been predestined to the plan of him who works all things in conformity with the purpose of his will in order that we, who were the first to hope in Christ might be *for the praise of his glory*" (v. 11-12).

"Having believed, you were marked in him with a seal, the promised Holy Spirit, who is a deposit guaranteeing our inheritance until the redemption of those who are God's possession—*to the praise of his glory*" (v. 13-14).

- *You are destined to be conformed to the image of Christ*—Romans 8:29

- *You are destined to stand firm in faith through trials.* As we mentioned earlier, Paul wrote the Thessalonians that we are destined for trials. But that is not all he writes. He wants us to know that we can stand firm in their faith through the trials (1 Thessalonians 3:2-3, 7-8, 10). No matter what you go through, you can make it. God gives you the grace to make it through the trials.

## *Your Calling Is a HARD-AND-FAST Calling*

Paul declares, "for God's gifts and call are irrevocable" (Romans 11:29). The King James Version translates it, "without repentance." This means that God is not going to change his mind. The context of this verse indicates that God's covenant is not negated by Israel's disobedience. God's gifts and calling for Israel were not revocable—they would not be negated or reversed. So also, we can apply the principle in the New Covenant—even when we blow it, God does not negate our calling. God's calling on our life is certain. It is hard and fast; it is durable; we can depend on it. We can depend on God. Paul assured, "If we are faithless, he will remain faithful" (2 Timothy 2:13).

Mark had blown it by deserting the ministry with Paul and Barnabas. And though, as a result, Paul had no use for Mark, Barnabas did not give up on him. He recognized that God still had a call on Mark's life, so he continued to mentor Mark. Eventually, God used Mark in mighty ways.

Paul later changed his mind, and wrote Timothy, "Get Mark and bring him with you, because he is helpful to me in my ministry" (2 Timothy 4:10).

Peter found him to be valuable, and took him on as his assistant, and under Peter's direction, he penned the Gospel of Mark, one of the four gospels that was canonized by the church as inspired by the Holy Spirit. Church history records that Mark became bishop of Alexandria, which became one of the most prominent centers of Christianity in the early church. Yes, Mark's calling was permanent, and so is yours. That calling may be expressed in different ways or phases, but God does not rescind His calling on your life. God will open for you doors that cannot be shut.

## ENLARGE YOUR TENTS

Pioneer missionary William Carey once declared, "Expect great things from God; do great things for God." Joshua was challenged by God that there was much more territory for the Israelites to possess (Joshua 13:1). There is much more territory God has for you. God exhorts us, "Enlarge the place of your tent, stretch your tent curtains wide, do not hold back; lengthen your cords, strengthen your stakes. For you will spread out to the right and to the left" (Isaiah 54:13-14). Expand your horizons to a higher and larger Christian life than you have experienced. A.B. Simpson challenges us to a "larger Christian life" in at least eight ways:

- A larger vision—Ephesians 1:17-19; 3:20-21
- A larger faith—Luke 17:5; 2 Pet. 1:5-8
- A larger love—1 Thessalonians 4:9-10; Ephesians 3:17-19
- A larger joy—Philippians 3:1; 4:4
- A larger experience—Philippians 3:10-14
- A larger work—Isaiah 54:2-3
- A larger hope—Romans 5:3-5
- A larger baptism in the Spirit—Ephesians 5:18

Read these Scripture verses above and meditate upon how you can be enlarged in each of these dimensions. Simpson enumerates five principles to becoming enlarged:

- Be delivered and lifted above old concepts, ideas, experiences, and your past.
- Be delivered from all human standards, opinions, and patterns.
- Accept all God sends to expand your spiritual life.

- Let the Holy Spirit work.
- Realize the magnitude of God. [98]

## TAKE THE PLUNGE

There comes a time to stop testing the waters with our toes, and instead become willing and determined to take the plunge and act in faith. Through poetic expression, A.B. Simpson encourages us to take the plunge by faith through the mercy of God to be all that God wants us to be and all that God wants us to do for His glory:

> The mercy of God is an ocean divine,
> A boundless and fathomless flood;
> Launch out in the deep, cut away the shoreline,
> And be lost in the mercy of God.
> Many, alas, only stand on the shore
>
> And gaze on the ocean so wide;
> They never have ventured its depths to explore
> Or to launch on the fathomless tide.
>
> Oh, let us launch out on this ocean so broad,
> Where floods of salvation e're flow;
> Oh, let us be lost in the mercy of God
> Till the depths of His fullness we know.

Once you have sought the Lord and received clearance from Him, you can find your niche by exploring the vast ocean of God Himself and His fullness of life and purpose.

## GO FORTH!

*"And say to Archippus, 'Take heed to the ministry which you have received in the Lord, that you may fulfill it'"*
(Colossians 4:17, NASB).

*"How long will you wait before you begin to take possession of the land that the Lord, the God of your fathers, has given you?"*
(Joshua 18:3).

There is a time to wait, but then there is a time to act. The old proverb says, "He who hesitates is lost." Paul exhorted Archippus to take heed to fulfill his calling. Joshua chided the Israelites for failing to possess fully the Promised Land. You may be waiting for God to do something, when God is waiting for you to do something.

Early in my adult life and ministry, I was not confident about knowing the will of God. Consequently, I became terribly indecisive in all areas of my life. It showed up frequently when my family would be on a long road trip. We would all be getting hungry, but we could not decide where to eat. I would say, "Where do you want to eat, honey?" And she would reply, "Wherever you want to eat." And we would go back and forth, "Well, I feel like this, but I am not up for that." And by the time we had made up our minds, we had missed the exit where the restaurants were!

Just as if we are hasty and get ahead of God, we miss His will, so if we hesitate in indecision, we can get behind God and miss His will. There is a time to step out by faith, saying, "Lord, I believe this is what you want for me. I will step out in faith. Show me if I am going astray." God does not want us to be passive. Passivity leads to paralysis.

As we are going, we can seek and discover God's will for our lives. Waiting on the Lord does not mean doing nothing. It means doing what we know to do, while anticipating God to speak and act on our behalf. We take a step, and God lights the way ahead of us. We entrust our steps to the Lord. Like an airline pilot who gets clearance from the tower to take off or land, especially in the dark, so when we get clearance from God we need not fear. It will be clear, it will not be groping in the dark. You have the signal and you have the lights in front of you. You can take off into God's purposes for your life.

Robert Schuller has an excellent motto for knowing when it is time to step out into God's purposes for our lives:

> When the idea is not right, God says, "NO!"
> When the time is not right, God says, "SLOW!"
> When we are not right, God says, "GROW!"
> When everything is right, God says, "GO!"[99]

There is a time for every purpose under heaven. Is it your time?

## FOR FURTHER REFLECTION

1. Describe how your calling is a high and heavenly calling.

2. How can you be enlarged in your vision and calling?

3. How is your destiny being worked out in your life?

4. In what ways can you launch out into more of what God desires you to be and to do?

5. What risks, doubts, or hesitations are holding you back? How can you deal with them and move on into what God has for you?

# Appendix

## ADDITIONAL RESOURCES FOR FINDING YOUR NICHE

### General Resources on Purpose

* Rick Warren, *The Purpose-Driven Life* (Grand Rapids: Zondervan, 2002)

  The best-selling general book on finding purpose in life.

* Erik Rees, *S.H.A.P.E.: Finding and Fulfilling Your Unique Purpose for Life* (Grand Rapids, MI: Zondervan, 2006).

  Expands on Rick Warren's five areas for discovering your purpose: spiritual gifts, heart, abilities, personality, and experiences.

* Tommy Barnett, *Reaching Your Dreams: 7 Steps for Turning Dreams into Reality.* Strang Communications, 2005.

  Barnett shows you how to follow the dreams God placed in your heart. Your purpose in life can only be made known as you pursue those dreams. Following each chapter are seven days of reflective questions and journaling exercises.

* Jane Kise and Kevin Johnson, *Find Your Fit: Dare to Act on God's Design for You.* Minneapolis: Bethany House Publishers, 1998.

  Guide for teens to discover their God-given uniqueness. Includes self-tests and inventories for discovering talents, spiritual gifts, values, and personality types.

### Resources for Discovering Your Spiritual Gifts

* C. Peter Wagner, Discover Your Spiritual Gifts (Ventura, CA: Regal Books, 2002, 2005).

  Includes The *Wagner-Modified Houts Spiritual Gifts Questionnaire*, one of the best-selling inventories on spiritual gifts.

- **J. Robert Clinton,** *Spiritual Gifts Manual* (Camp Hill, PA: Horizon Books, 1985).

  This is perhaps the most comprehensive study of all the spiritual gifts listed or implied in the Bible.

- **Bill Gothard,** *Institute in Basic Life Principles: Advanced Seminar*

  Gothard's Advanced Seminar contains a section on discovering motivational gifts.

- **Don and Katie Fortune**—*Discover Your God-given Gifts.* (Grand Rapids, MI: Chosen Books, 1987).

  This is my favorite motivational gifts survey. It includes gift testing for children and youth and a vocational guide for each gift area and/or combination of gifts.

## Vocational/Career Resources

- **Bob Buford,** *Halftime: Changing Your Game Plan from Success to Significance.* Grand Rapids, MI: Zondervan, 1994.

  Discusses issues and changes surrounding midlife and focuses on living for significance rather that success in the second half of life.

- **John Bradley, with Dave and Neta Jackson,** *Switching Tracks: Advancing Through Five Crucial Phases of Your Career.* Grand Rapids, MI: Fleming H. Revell, 1994.

- **IDAK Career Match** www.idakgroup.com

  Inventory often used in Christian and secular organizations to identify personal assessment of interests, values and natural talents. Career match print out reports provide recommended organizations and detailed descriptions, as well as up to five titles within each type of organization that appear to fit one's natural talents,preferences, priorities, and values.

- **Life Pathways/Career Direct. Lee Ellis,** *The Pathfinder: A Guide to Career Decision Making.* Gainesville, GA: Life Pathways/ Christian Financial Concepts, 2000.

Career planning manual. Used by college and university Career Planning and Placement offices with their incoming students to assess path for majors and for graduating students to provide vocational planning and guidance.

## *Personality Profiles*

- **Styles of Influence Questionaire**. Center for Church Renewal, Plano, Texas

  Helps to understand your personal leadership style of influence: cognitive (how we think about and evaluate our world), relational (how we relate to others emotionally), goal achievement (how we relate to others to accomplish a task), detail (how we prefer to handle details). This is a self-administered questionnaire.

The following are personality and vocational inventories, usually administered by someone who has been trained and certified in this type of training:

- **L-E-A-D Personality Inventory**. Walter A. Lacey and John J. Fanning, *L-E-A-D Personality Inventory* (Forest, VA: Church Growth Institute, 1986).

- **Gary Smalley Personality Tests**. See online at:: www.smalleyonline.com/assessments/personalitytest.html and www.smalleyonline.com/articles/i_discoveringpersonality.html.

- **Myers-Briggs Type Indicator** (MBTI).

  Inventory often used in Christian colleges and graduate schools as well as Christian and secular organizations to identify personal styles and preferences, including four basic mental functions or processes: sensing or observing, intuition, thinking, and feeling; as well as four basic attitudes toward life: introversion, extroversion, judgment (decision-making, organizing and planning), and perception. These are organized into 16 types that identify our locus of energy, what we pay attention to, how we make decisions, and the way we choose to live.

## Mentoring, Coaching, and Spiritual Direction

- **Bob Logan and Sherilyn Carlton,** *Coaching 101.* St. Charles, IL: Church Smart Resources, 2003.

- www.thechristiancoach.com

- www.christiancoaches.org

- **Gordon F. Shea,** *Making the Most of Being Mentored: How to Grow from a Mentoring Partnership.* Crisp Publications, 1999.

- **Tom Pace with Walter Jenkins,** *Mentor: The Kid and the CEO.* Edmond, OK: Mentor Hope Publishing, 2007.

- **Alan Jones,** *Exploring Spiritual Direction.* Cambridge, MA: Cowley Publishing, 1999.

- **Jeannette A. Bakke,** *Holy Invitations: Exploring Spiritual Direction.* Grand Rapids, MI: Baker Books, 2000.

- **Keith Anderson and Andy Reese,** *Spiritual Mentoring: A Guide for Seeking and Giving Direction.* Downers Grove, IL: InterVarsity, 1999.

## Resources for Developing Vision

- **Andy Stanley,** *Visioneering: God's Blueprint for Developing and Maintaining Vision.* Sisters, OR: Multnomah Press, 1999

- **George Barna,** *The Power of Vision.* Ventura, CA: Regal Books, 1999, 2003.

- **Myles Munroe,** *The Principles and Power of Vision: Keys to Achieving Personal and Corporate Destiny.* New Kensington, PA: Whitaker, 2003.

# Notes

1   A.W. Tozer, *Born After Midnight* (Harrisburg, PA: Christian Publications, 1959), 44.
2   Neil T. Anderson, *Living Free in Christ* (Ventura, CA: Regal Books, 1993); Neil T. Anderson, *Victory over the Darkness* (Ventura, CA: Regal Books, 1990).
3   Anderson, *Living Free in Christ*, 11.
4   Ibid., 278.
5   Paul E. Billheimer, *Don't Waste Your Sorrows* (Ft. Washington, PA: Christian Literature Crusade, 1977), 35.
6   Oswald Chambers, *My Utmost for His Highest* (New York, NY: Dodd, Mead and Co., 1935), Oct. 19.
7   Ibid., July 10, July 11.
8   Ibid.
9   F. Brook, "My Goal Is God Himself," *Hymns of the Christian Life* (Harrisburg, PA: Christian Publications, 1978), 265.
10   Chambers, *My Utmost for His Highest*, Mar. 17.
11   Oswald Chambers, *Run Today's Race* (United Kingdom: Marshall Morgan & Scott, 1968), May.
12   Clinton Arnold, *Three Crucial Questions about Spiritual Warfare* (Grand Rapids: Baker, 1997), 66.
13   Mark Pearson, *Christian Healing* (Lake Mary, FL: Charisma House, 2004), 262-263.
14   A.C. Palmer, "Ready," *Hymns of the Christian Life* (Harrisburg, PA: Christian Publications, 1978), 465.
15   Paul L. King, *Moving Mountains: Lessons in Bold Faith from Great Evangelical Leaders* (Grand Rapids, MI: Chosen Books, 2004).
16   Cited in Bill Gothard, *The Power of Crying Out* (Sisters, OR: Multnomah Publishers, 2002), 74.
17   A.W. Tozer, *The Root of the Righteous* (Camp Hill, PA: Christian Publications, 1955, 1986), 153.
18   Oswald Chambers, *God's Workmanship* (Grand Rapids: Discovery House Publishers, 1953, 1997), 81.
19   From the website: http://www.charm.net/~totoro/doula.html. See Marshall H. Klaus, John H. Kennell, Phyllis H. Klaus, *Mothering the Mother: How a Doula Can Help You Have a Shorter, Easier, and Healthier Birth* (New York: Perseus Books, 1993).(New York: Perseus Books, 1993).

20  James W. Garrett, *The Doulos Principle* (Tulsa, OK: Doulos Publishing, 1999), 12-16.

21  Ibid., 25.

22  Ibid., 25-38.

23  Ibid., 41, 49, 57, 67, 69, 77.

24  Garrett, 42.

25  Chambers, *My Utmost for His Highest*, May 25.

26  Richard Foster, *Celebration of Discipline* (San Francisco, CA: HarperSanFrancisco, 1978, 1988), 161.

27  Oswald Chambers, *Called of God*, (United Kingdom: Marshall Morgan & Scott, 1936), *The Complete Works of Oswald Chambers* (Grand Rapids: Discovery House, 2000), 252.

28  David Henderson, "Teaching a Church to Pray," *Leadership*, Fall 2001, 47.

29  Peter Nanfelt, "The Profitable Path," *Missions Update*, The Christian and Missionary Alliance, November 2002.

30  Bob Buford, *Halftime: Changing Your Game Plan from Success to Significance* (Grand Rapids, MI: Zondervan, 1994), 112-113.

31  A. B. Simpson, "The Power of Stillness," *Alliance Weekly*, April 16, 1916, 21.

32  Paul E. Billheimer, *Adventure in Adversity* (Wheaton: Tyndale House, 1984), 12.

33  Amy Carmichael, *Thou Givest. . . They Gather* (Fort Washington, PA: Christian Literature Crusade, 1958), 110.

34  Cited in John Eldridge, *Wild at Heart* (Nashville, TN: Thomas Nelson, 2001), 197.

35  See 2 Samuel 7.

36  Chambers, *Called of God, The Complete Works of Oswald Chambers*, 264.

37  Cited in J. Oswald Sanders, *Spiritual Leadership* (Chicago, IL: Moody Press, 1967, 1980, 1994), 57.

38  Some from a business background may say, "This looks like MBO (Management By Objective)." Well, it is MBO—Ministry by Objective! God thought of it millennia before the business world got hold of it. The business world just discovered valid, ancient principles that come from Scripture.

39  Robert H. Schuller, *You Can Become the Person You Want to Be* (Old Tappan, NJ: Fleming H. Revell, 1973), 86.

40  Eldridge, 137-138.

41   Stephen Arterburn, *Reframe Your Life: Transforming Your Pain into Purpose* (New York: FaithWords, 2007).

42   From the pamphlet by Robert Hillyer, "Set Free: Testimony of Robert Hillyer."

43   Sandra Clifton, *From New Age to New Life* (Lake Mary, FL: Creation House, 2007).

44   Gene McMath, *Twice Rescued: A New View of Life from the Bottom of the Cliff* (Tulsa, OK: Word and Spirit Press, 2007).

45   Quoted from *The Motto Calendar*, Douglassville, PA, September 2002.

46   Watchman Nee, *The Normal Christian Life* (London: Victory Press, 1957), 154-158, 165, 169-179.

47   Alan Redpath, *Victorious Christian Living* (Westwood, NJ: Fleming H. Revell, 1955), 27.

48   Chambers, *My Utmost for His Highest*, June 13.

49   Oswald Chambers, *Our Brilliant Heritage*, (United Kingdom: Marshall Morgan & Scott, 1965), *The Complete Works of Oswald Chambers*, 947.

50   These characteristics are adapted primarily from teachings of Bill Gothard, Advanced Seminar, Institute in Basic Youth Conflicts, and Don and Katie Fortune, *Discover Your God-Given Gifts* (Grand Rapids, MI: Chosen Books, 1987).

51   Don and Katie Fortune, 235, 243.

52   Tim LaHaye, *Spirit-Controlled Temperament* (Wheaton, IL: Tyndale House Publishers, 1966), 126.

53   Walter A. Lacey and John J. Fanning, *L-E-A-D Personality Inventory* (Forest, VA: Church Growth Institute, 1986).

54   Adapted from the following sources: Professor Carol Blan, Doctor of Ministry lectures, Oral Roberts University, 1997, and from Bruce W. Jones, *Ministerial Leadership in a Managerial World*, 1988; Doges and Braund, *Understanding How Others Misunderstand You*, 1998.

55   For a survey of many of these, see Bruce W. Jones, *Ministerial Leadership in a Managerial World.*, Doges and Braund, *Understanding How Others Misunderstand You*. Others include *TJTA* (Taylor-Johnson Temperament Analysis), Robert Dale's *Minister-Leaders, California Psychology Inventory* (CPI); *L-E-A-D Personality Inventory*, produced for Church Growth Institute by Interlink Consultants, Ltd., 1986, 1994.

56   See his personality tests and descriptions at: www.smalleyonline.com/assessments/personalitytest.html and www.smalleyonline.com/articles/i_discoveringpersonality.html.

57  LaHaye, *Spirit-Controlled Temperaments*, 126-141.
58  Lewis Drummond, *Spurgeon: Prince of Preachers* (Grand Rapids, MI: Kregel, 1992), 91.
59  Foster, *Celebration of Discipline*, 175.
60  See Bruce E. Olsen, *Bruchko* (Carol Stream, IL: Creation House, 1973, 1978).
61  George Müller, *The Autobiography of George Müller* (Springdale, PA: Whitaker Books, 1984), 171-172, 175.
62  Quoted in Sanders, *Spiritual Leadership*, 45.
63  Chambers, *My Utmost for His Highest*, Oct. 17.
64  Chambers, *My Utmost for His Highest*, Nov. 10.
65  Frank Houghton, *Amy Carmichael of Dohnavur*, 78.
66  Oswald Chambers, *My Utmost for His Highest*, Aug. 10.
67  Oswald Chambers, *The Servant as His Lord*, (United Kingdom: Marshall Morgan & Scott, 1959), *The Complete Works of Oswald Chambers*, 1284.
68  Oswald Chambers, *He Shall Glorify Me* (Grand Rapids: Discovery House, 1946, 1993), 262.
69  Buford, *Halftime*, 70.
70  Schuller, 150.
71  Chambers, *My Utmost for His Highest*, Aug. 30.
72  John Bradley with Dave and Neta Jackson, *Switching Tracks: Advancing Through Five Crucial Phases of Your Career* (Grand Rapids, MI: Fleming H. Revell, 1994), 13-17.
73  Jamie Buckingham, *A Way Through the Wilderness* (Old Tappan, NJ: Fleming H. Revell/Chosen Books, 1986), 22.
74  Buckingham, *A Way Through the Wilderness*, x, xv.
75  Renzo Fidani, "He Brought Us Out," ZionSong Music, Orlando, FL, 1983. Used by permission.
76  Billheimer, *Don't Waste Your Sorrows*, 10.
77  Billheimer, *Adventure in Adversity*, 98.
78  Buckingham, *A Way Through the Wilderness*, 45.
79  Cited in Sanders, *Spiritual Leadership*, 150-151.
80  Sanders, *Spiritual Leadership*, 28-29.
81  Chambers, *Called of God, The Complete Works of Oswald Chambers*, 262.
82  Redpath, 69-70.
83  Fenelon, *Let Go* (Springdale, PA: Whitaker House, 1973), 8-9.
84  Chambers, *Called of God, The Complete Works of Oswald Chambers*, 262.

85  *World Shapers* (Wheaton: Harold Shaw Publishers, 1991), 106.

86  Richard J. Foster, *Prayer: Finding the Heart's True Home* (San Francisco: HarperSanFrancisco, 1992), 17, 18.

87  Annie Johnson Flint, "Pressed," *Poems That Preach* (Wheaton, IL: Sword of the Lord Publishers, 1952), #60. Public domain.

88  Bradley, 189.

89  S.I. McMillen, *None of These Diseases* (Old Tappan, NJ: Fleming H. Revell, 1963), 62.

90  Dallas Willard, *The Divine Conspiracy* (San Francisco: HarperSanFrancisco, 1997), 233.

91  Charles Paul Conn, cited in Ted W. Engstrom, *Pursuit of Excellence* (Grand Rapids: Zondervan, 1982), 21.

92  John C. Maxwell, *Developing the Leader Within You* (Nashville: Thomas Nelson, 1993), 161.

93  Foster, *Celebration of Discipline*, 80.

94  Ibid., 90-95.

95  A. B. Simpson, *Christ in the Bible* (Camp Hill, PA: Christian Publications, 1992), 6:206.

96  Maxwell, *Developing the Leader Within You*, 202.

97  See Paul F. Schmidt, *Coping with Difficult People* (Philadelphia, PA: Westminster Press, 1980).

98  A. B. Simpson, *A Larger Christian Life* (Camp Hill, PA: Christian Publications, 1988), 51-65.

99  Schuller, 150.